*New & *
Poem

for Louis and Patrick and Max

New & Selected Poems

Lauris Edmond

BLOODAXE BOOKS

ISBN: 1 85224 181 0

First published 1992 by
Bloodaxe Books Ltd,
P.O. Box 1SN,
Newcastle upon Tyne NE99 1SN.

Published simultaneously in
New Zealand by Oxford University Press.

Bloodaxe Books Ltd acknowledges
the financial assistance of Northern Arts.

ACKNOWLEDGEMENTS
Acknowledgements are due to Mallinson Rendel,
who published *Wellington Letter*; to Pegasus Press, who
published *The Pear Tree*; and to the editors of the following
publications in which some recent poems have appeared:
London Magazine, Meanjin, New Zealand Listener, PN Review,
and *Westerly*. The author gratefully acknowledges
the assistance of the New Zealand Literary Fund.

Cover designed by Fay McAlpine.
Typesetting by Sovereign Print, Christchurch, New Zealand.
Printed in Hong Kong.

Contents

From *In Middle Air*

Moonshine Valley

Wild grasses I know you, let me come in,
cocksfoot and clover, prairie grass, fennel and rye,
give me a good place to lie
here in the hillside's hollow
full of green smells and heat,
and the buzz of the earth's brain
ruminating away beneath
grasses singing old earth rolling rolling
and the Rimutakas riding their blue horses on the sky.

Brown top, featherhead, plantain and cutty grass,
a dozen yards to the dog daisies
beside the dry stones of the road;
and the wind heading on up the valley,
crossing to Moonshine,
over the mountains and north
to the Wairarapa's sun-dazed plains
grasses singing old earth rolling rolling
and the Rimutakas riding their blue horses on the sky.

Nowhere to go, the road all dust and danger,
houses full of grief, and quarrelling
in the hot street of the town –
come take me you wild warm grasses
hide me an hour or so
from the world's sickness, drown
its cries with your resonant harmonies
grasses singing old earth rolling rolling
and the Rimutakas riding their blue horses on the sky.

11

Boy

Put him near the front, they said, *watch him –*
a foreigner, something of a misfit . . .
Is that all? Not quite; more than mere
position he needs space: obstructions rise
to meet his wandering boot, books drop,
his omnipresent elbows prod, quite
by accident, his neighbour – most
fall back, the boys discreet in jerseys,
certainly the top-knot tossing girls;
all prefer less random battlefields.

Concentration fitful – and indeed
his dreams take him where space is less a problem:
the wide wind-ridden skies of his native
Lithuania pour distances
into his mind. Now he wakes in a raw
King Country cottage, sees the railway spin
its silver thread across the hills; he wrote,
once, 'My pa drives a jigger, sometimes
at dawn I see the mountains burn with beauty.'
Good God what is he – a budding Nabokov?

Well, that cannot save him, if he is,
the malice of a taunting crowd around
the school – or later, on the logging track
a punch-up every week or two from hostile
ugly gangs. Sad, but let's not worry
overmuch – he's ours, he'll roughen up.

The day's not far off when his splendid mountains,
their fires all put out, will look on him
taking his fist to another puzzled stranger,
some lad who needs to learn he's not like us.

Waterfall

I do not ask for youth, nor for delay
in the rising of time's irreversible river
that takes the jewelled arc of the waterfall
in which I glimpse, minute by glinting minute,
all that I have and all I am always losing
as sunlight lights each drop fast, fast falling.

I do not dream that you, young again,
might come to me darkly in love's green darkness
where the dust of the bracken spices the air
moss, crushed, gives out an astringent sweetness
and water holds our reflections
motionless, as if for ever.

It is enough now to come into a room
and find the kindness we have for each other
– calling it love – in eyes that are shrewd
but trustful still, face chastened by years
of careful judgment; to sit in the afternoons
in mild conversation, without nostalgia.

But when you leave me, with your jauntiness
sinewed by resolution more than strength
– suddenly then I love you with a quick
intensity, remembering that water,
however luminous and grand, falls fast
and only once to the dark pool below.

August, Ohakune

All night in winter the dogs howled
up the hill in the mad woman's house –
she had forty living inside,
half starved, truculent, snarling

at all who came; but only kids
would creep along the derelict track:
half choked with fear they stalked phantoms,
found their nightmare, an ancient stag,
eyeless, ghastly holes gouged
by rats, above the blackened door.
They smothered screams – and went back,
in daylight only . . .
                              Further off
we could hear the river
intermittently tapping its menacing morse
and the morepork call through the dark;
at last the frost hunted us in
to take shelter in a cold uneasy sleep.

Over all was the mountain, Snow Queen
of an old tale, brilliant and deadly, brooding
on the fate of frozen villages.

Before a Funeral

The great bright leaves have fallen
outside your window
they lie about
torn by the season from
the beggared cherry trees.
In your room, alone,
I fold and hide away
absurd, unnecessary things –
your books, still ready and alert,
it seems, for understanding,
clothes, dry and cold,
surprised in holding still
to hairs upon the collars,
handkerchiefs in pockets,
socks, awry, not ready for
the queer neglect of death.

14

Mechanically useful, I make
preparations for some possible
impossible journey no one
will ever take; work will help
they tell me, and indeed
your room is now nothing
but things, and tidy.
I have put away your life.

Out in the autumn garden
a sharp rapacious wind
snatches the brilliant booty
of the leaves. The blackened branches
groan. They knot, and hold.
And yet the cold will come.

Ohakune Fires

There were bonfires on the hillsides
in those days, high
above the raw-boned town
and trees and men giants against the sky
grappling for mastery – not men but bushmen took
their slashers in to hack
blazes on the beech trunks
smacking up a track of sorts,
forced a way to the ridge and stood
straight up to breast the trees
defeated, famished
in the thinning air.

Back on the farm on milder hills
they clubbed second growth
and lit their necessary fires;
women came – sometimes a child
screaming when the blazing
raced up close.

          Dark, and
the booze began, tall tales
of men and bullocks gulped down
in twenty feet of mud, or some
such thing, in grandad's roaring time.
Round them the spit and snore
of logs' red bodies,
later the blundering
journey home (one, a neighbour,
drunken-drowned in the freezing stream).
And all the time
the hard stars riding by.

Time, it's a moving stage –
bonfires still blaze
and we hold out our hands
across a widening space
calling, hearing now only
the faint snap of the burning
and the far-off pack-a-pack
of the axes.

Late Starling

Yes yes of course I am hard to please –
yet I can see this quiet sky
with the evening in it
and that poised drop of darkness
the late starling
that comes to the dead peak
of the old pine. Yes, and taste too
the tart smoke of the leaves,
ghost of the year's green,
observe Tortle the cat
slow-stepping across
the darkening grass,
and the single golden pear,
huge and alone, that hangs like a yellow
lantern on its bare branch.

16

Once we would have stood, my hand in yours,
quiet too, and full of wonder –
was it spring, perhaps, those other evenings?
I have forgotten.
I only know that we have come
to quarrelling, and not even this
communicable peace
can speak to us now.

The Affair

We discuss important matters
but naturally do not speak
the words that shout
behind our eyes;
everything would be too little
to say. Or too much.

Why are we not astonished
at ourselves
at each other?
Why are we always making adjustments?
Why do we not admit
that great dragons with heavy-lidded eyes
come up out of the sea
and stand over us, weeping
when we laugh softly
in the darkness?

I wish we were not so sophisticated,
I wish we could make scenes
be badly dressed, argue,
have no taste in wine;
I am full of screaming
but my voice is low and elegant;
when the moonlight falls
on your carved face

there is a sound of birds singing
outside the window
when you close the shutter
I know how to conceal my terror.

We have grown small
as jewelled crustaceans
holding to our rock
making imperceptible
but charming gestures;
our style is the envy of our friends.
Only we can hear the echo of caverns
behind our brilliant eyes
as the wind cries along the shore.

Scar Tissue

Wellington is an old crone
all gaps, teeth knocked out;
daily, watchers stare
at waving arms that claw
walls into rubble.
A case of indecent exposure
occurred last week:
bed, wardrobe, blue wallpaper
swinging high – drunken, ridiculous,
skin peeled off and bricks falling
into the crawling pit where puddles show
the sea still seeps under the Quay.

I used to walk this way on windy nights
past Barretts' roaring doorway
stinking of beer and early closing
up the old steps, not then assaulted
by the big drills, nor lit
by simpering shops,
but dark, clay-smelling, convolvulus
and periwinkle sprawling on the stones

and fennel, ripe and strong,
grasping the bank. There,
a few yards from the rattling trams,
I would come to you, breathless from running;
I remember the wind wrapping us,
your hands cold inside my coat
and the shreds of our voices whirled up up high
into a torn corner of sky.

Long afterwards I still was shaken
when I passed, the bitter wind could still
sting me to tears. But no more –
a pulse has dulled in the flesh;
I feel it less.
Today they've got a new instrument,
a great iron ball that smashes at
the city's trembling past.
I gape with the rest, say
with the same dull voice I know
it has to go.

Leaving

Clouds wrangle in a windy sky,
beside me willows scatter
fretful patterns on the water;
the day, the year, ten years, are blown away
leaving only a grain or two of sand
under the eyelid of the mind.

Yesterday to walk by the autumn lake
was to sing in the swing of the year; today I come
detached, dispossessed, neutral, numb;
my dream is full of strangers – when I wake
they will conspire to seem
my friends. But I will long for home.

Piano Practice

Child, creature, little anxious girl,
your whole body frowns,
your clambering hands
grapple mountains. The rocky crotchets mass
above you, and suspense hangs
on quavering slopes
past the next hard turning.
Your tense legs work, shoulders lean
towards higher ground – not much further –
when you can reach the last
black ominous chord, *sforzando*,
octaves on the left like boulders rolling,
at last – you're there!

Summit achieved, you butterfly about,
the sunny day breaks out and everything
is sharp and singing.
Released, you run down the hill
to where the green-gold gorse waits
to force its stinging kisses
on your small hard shins.

Sunday Night

The day recedes within the dying fire,
its fragile facade still perfect
but like curtains in forgotten rooms
that crumble at a finger's touch
a shape of dust. The children sleep.
Surrendering action I contract
inwardly, leaving the blank outline
of a silhouette. The closing of doors
and putting out of lights extinguishes
more than a room. What is a woman that she
should wake and sleep in other people's lives?
Time passing in silence touches
the unresisting embers into ash.

Ponies

This morning, out early, I was confronted
by horses – two, then four –
coming from nowhere, head-high
along the street, their rhythmic pacing
and muscled sheen of hips and hocks
making patterns – dance drama
with sunlight – shrinking houses and hedges
till the whole block burgeoned out
into foothills, ranges and tussocky plains.

Behind them came the shadows
of little long-ago ponies,
noses into the wind, rough-coated
brumbies wearing their last freedom
galloping down ridges and away
over the wind-whistling plateau
of Tauranga-Taupo, more than
half a hundred years ago.

Two Birth Poems

1. A Shift of Emphasis

Do not come too close, nor touch
the swollen knot
that tightens round
my multiplicities of pain;
that scream that flies about the room
is mine. I allowed it out.
Keep off. Join the mice in nice
white uniforms running about
with their routines.

It happens here. All my eyes glare,
a thousand fists fight
in the raging darkness of my body –
this smothered yell
comes to kill.
Look out! It cracks me open, it is
the axe that splits the skull –

the knot of blood is cut.
I am broken, scattered,
fragments of me melt and flow –
I am not here; gravity's red centre
has slipped; off course, I roll about
like wind-blown eggshells.

Cradled in the world's lap lies instead
a tiny grey-faced rag of flesh
with a cry as thin as muslin,
and all the power to possess the earth
curled up behind the blindness of its eyes.

2. *Zero Population Growth*

It was the anonymity I noticed first –
the flowers and I both languishing
in unlit corridors,
banished for recalcitrant
behaviour, minor problems
for the management.

A kind carnation said
'Your water's leaking dear,
you'll have your baby long before the morning.'
But still the teacups chattered
while a yellow string of light remained in place
between the supper cups
and our disgrace.

Then a big pain bowled me,
I reeled, sprawled –
Heavens! it would not do!
A flock of nurses flew
to peck protestingly
at a wavering whale
impaled on a lino square.
Even the flowers disdained to smile.

I became incorrigibly plural –
there seemed no end to limbs and things
I could produce; the refuse disposal squad
briskly dismantled, finally towed away
the remains, still seething;
beside me a strange animal
in a basket, breathing.

Later I noticed a small sardonic smile
on the curtain, having a swing;
it chirped 'You've done it.
You clever thing.'

Sunday Morning

Down at the corner dairy
the Sunday morning sun
is yellow as a pancake
frying on the sky;
last night's litter
shuffles about in a gutter
and the seedy little shop
stands up and wipes its chin
ready for the day's
business to begin.

It's all old codgers at first,
forgot the milk, out of fags,

wanting, in all cynicism,
the Sunday papers, not liking
the girlies but liking less
to miss them, scratching old itches,
lingering, fidgeting . . .
Then the kids, shoved out
of tousled kitchens for bread
baked beans spaghetti, pinching
the change for a coke, grinning
all over, playing games, loving it,
sure, little sods, of their indestructible
Sunday selves.

Later the marvellous girls
shiny and slow dressed in sex
full enough to spill
of last night's loving,
on their lips the sly taste of the morning –
and the boys, off-hand and matey,
eyes on the weather, ready
to roll up the day, stow in
the boot, nothing doing
around here, get what's left
of Saturday's grog bugger off
leave boredom behind.

And they go – cars hot,
sliding past polished like buns
straight out of summer's oven;
where is it, the sun-drumming
dazzle they're after? Who knows –
not us – it's anywhere but here.

From *The Pear Tree*

Time of Silence

Tomorrow I will remember you
and my own good behaviour, understand
your child is sick, work difficult
your money spent; tonight there can be
no words. She is dead and I am lost
in grief for her, and nothing
I might do for her or you
can change it now.

In the morning I will be resolute
responsible as to your claims
rational, moderate; tonight
I know only that she has gone
into the darkness alone
though I cried out to hold her close
and not one of you
can tell me otherwise.

I will have no telling of any kind, none;
do not say there is work to be done, explanations
made, that spring will follow even this
savage winter – perhaps perhaps; tonight
I do not care. There is only the wind's door
through which she has gone and the sound
of an irredeemable silence out of which
she will never speak again.

The Pear Tree

Pear tree like snow blowing across the sunlight:
spring this year is not for love, nor hope,
nor passion, but something with which we are to be
reconciled. I remember the winter tree,
its bare branches entwined in the hieroglyphics
of a message too hard for us to comprehend,
a language of defeat.

Yesterday I saw the first green swellings
and a green shadow over the fallen husks
of bark shredded by weather in a winter
that brought death to the house – a bleak time
when frost blackened the geraniums, so
indestructibly scarlet last autumn;
sap was low and the cracked shell of the pear
tree promised nothing. We had so little
force or fibre, the numb days when
we sat together, pain like a blight
withering our understanding, and the dark arms
of the tree lifted across the window
as if in supplication for us.

Now the thousand faces of spring shake
their white light across the glass; in us
too there is a stirring, of force or feeling –
but this is no simple flowering, no ordered season;
the hard grind of grief still holds,
a bitter sap in the wood blurring the break
of the season. No spring can restore to her the changes
of sun and rain, the quiver of wind in the blossom
the morning's tender sky; her sleep is unshakeable
beyond all seasons. We must make alone what sense of this
we can. Spring is a reckoning.

3 A.M.

I remember the last red rose
and that it darkened a little
every day, drawing into itself
almost black at the end in its
bright green bottle
on the white sill by the kitchen window,
and the winter weather waning
the garden greening, beyond –
I remember it died, months ago.

The last hard clasp of hands
and the standing together
in the blue winter twilight
with infinite gentleness talking
inconsequentially through
someone's silent weeping – that too
is over; we scattered long ago
to our afternoon houses
to work and to sleep.

But the night is querulous and full
of arrangements; composing
answers to letters, remembering
obligations, I am held as
at a dull meeting; dry-eyed,
tired-minded, I hear no voices
but the night wind
meddling at the silence.

In a great sorrow we are helpless:
children, we trust the pitiless stars
to lead us by the hand; this small
darkness is a shut room.
It is not pain we fear, but triviality.

The Third Person

I do not know how to describe the third person but
on days when the doves came hurtling over the city
flung upwards in great purring armfuls outside your window
and fell, piling like black hail on ledges of buildings
across the street, he came in, he was there – let us
call him a man. He preened his purple feathers.

His eyes were brilliant, unblinking; he became
servant, interpreter, master and miracle-maker,
intricate designer of harmony out of
our broken fragments of love and confusion; I thought
you had summoned him for me, understanding
my weakness. I found him beautiful.

I came to you one cold evening in April,
the summer doves had flown, you were busy;
in the hard blue light the third person was very tall
and sharpened his steely claws meticulously.
When I showed my fear you moved slowly to stand beside him
and stared at me calmly without recognition.

Rodin Sculptures

Unexpectedly, they were no greater
than life size, smaller in fact, not curious
nor quaint; this was a weekday lunch hour
Wellington tossing its sun among
the sauntering crowd, a room
and these figures occupying it.

Yet to stand close was to feel in each
an intensity so fierce you had to step back
pain struck so deep

the abandonment dislodged each foothold
the muscles of every back
ached in its eloquence –

surely some huge act, earth movement of the mind,
condensed the wide meanderings of dreaming
into these nuggets of life, breath made solid,
as cosmic pressure draws a great star
into the compass of a single rock
of black and unimaginable density.

Kinekis: A Performance

Life can be endured all right, but art –
it is terrifying; it admits no compromise
no falling from an exact position: the dancer's
hand, now, across his face warding off evil
while a cold strictness keeps him still – if he
were real someone would lie to him, say it's all right;
but he is an artist and alone. He thrusts
me into the night to beat and howl.

As for the clown gaping from his huge
white mask, making frantic gestures, sagging
in his old man's body – is there no one about
who is worse off even than he? I cannot
help, I find him hateful; I have dressed
to come here. His insistent reminders
destroy my defences.

But then there is the singer whimsically
strumming that 'love is like tobacco' – he
surely would not frighten anyone. No?
He is worst of all; he persuades us
he is real, tells great lies and all the time
he knows he's not to be believed.

A Desirable Property on an Elevated Section

I think today that violent men should live
on hillsides; they would find, as I do, there
is no losing of your temper here,
the land will not allow it. It will receive
you on its own conditions; yes, come
close, take off, if you must, this old coat
of ivy, slash it, trample it underfoot;
but after (the message is polite but firm),

when the vine's white wrenched hands lie
tangled, nothing now to hold, and you
bring out your scraps – rosemary, a new
gazania – pretty things, you say,
to decorate more suitably that
naked knuckled clay – do not suppose
that all decisions to be made are yours
(an illusion one may hold where land is flat).

There will be no fuss; but if you press
intruding hands too far, expect to lay
the ghosts of that forbidding privacy,
they exact the price of all possessiveness:
drive deep, nudge and nuzzle as you will
towards an insistent intimacy; the hard
and unpersuaded clay, clod by clod,
will turn its back on you and slip downhill.

Turning the Pear Tree to Paper

Towards evening on a still and colourless Sunday
– and winter coming on – before the late tray of tea
brings us from other rooms or the garden, somebody
mentions lighting the fire and a neighbour perhaps calls . . .

30

there is a time when time itself comes to nothing,
light on the wall stares without expression,
a mere absence of darkness; chair, table,
flower become outlines as words repeated lose meaning;
the harbour is sealed, an opaque window at the end
of the world, and a dog barking far off tapping at it –
I too am weightless, a leaf's skeleton, dry
and pale, all green flesh eaten by worms that came
to the autumn garden and turned the pear tree to paper.

But a great silent horseman lifting his hooves comes riding
across the sky; we tremble, and are saved by our fear.
Now we can hurry in to stand together
and talk with quick hopefulness, waiting
for evening to fall, remembering what we are
and peering into the shadows to try to make out
the tremulous existences of others.

The Conformist

Sparrows early on the road walk
staccato poised as courtiers;
the morning is royal blue.

It lies among the mountains across
the water and watches from sleep
the jewelled mask of the sea.

I must be nimble as the sparrows,
as scrupulous as to protocol
as brief – I will strut and serve

protecting myself with my duties but
keeping my secret desire
awake till nightfall

because I wish to come very close
to know the slow movement from
the mountain, to lie with the beast

in the treacherous waters of the afternoon
to hear the scavenging gulls scream
above my closed eyes

and in the evening to take my knife
with the curved blade and handle of kauri
– and after the act to walk

into a night of dry sand and look back
at the spreading shadow of blood
not my own.

Eden Cultivated

Think of her coming in from the garden,
her hair blowing and the green breath
of summer drifting across the verandah
– the long grass, and the smell of apples –
behind her a blazing February sky,
the first thistledowns, and the haze;
see her drag out the old capacious
preserving pan from the darkened pantry
smelling of spices and orange peel,
and notice the small lines round her eyes,
the bones of her bending shoulders . . .
and wait – for how do you know, this time,
if she will offer you one apple
or many, or possibly none at all?

Mother to Daughter

Last year, last week, this morning
even, you turned to me
as to a remedy,
well tried, for an old malady;

Here at the open window
'You will know what to do' you said
'Tell me, reassure me, as always – '
As always, I understood.

Above us the sycamore (last year
so slight, so slender) elbowed
its way up, heavy and high –
ten feet more of it this year
crowding into the sky –

we talked; my old tale followed
its customary course:
it pleased me. Then I saw you
shrug despairingly
and turn away in tears,
perhaps of exasperation.

All your child's life
I prepared with care
the ground for every new growth;
nothing prepared me
for the first small death,
that I should be so shaken
by its sudden thrust of pain.

All Possession is Theft

There had been rain in the morning and a chaffinch,
before we surprised it, strutted beside a pool
on the lawn; the house was white, polite, had nothing
to say, but the trees – the great, well-heeled, patrician
trees – turned their green shoulders aside;
the pohutukawa has lineage, I would be certain
to make faux pas across its genealogies.
And my foot slipped between clay and concrete,
a magpie jeered and left, noisily.
The land agent drooled his obsequies – the previous
occupant, a psychiatrist . . . I thought I saw him

at the window frowning over his sad case histories,
neglecting his paths but cared for by his trees;
and touched one, tentatively, found instead
its green shawl of long three-fingered leaves,
a pink flower luxurious as an orchid, and in
the shadow a single fruit, narrow, golden,
the poised and secret guardian of an old season's
accumulations. 'Banana passion fruit'
– the agent, natural for a moment, pressed on
'The elevation here . . . ' I turned aside
breathless, feeling faintly lecherous, closed
my hand about that small old bag of gold
and, with a quick tug, took it. I live here now.

Minas

Sunset comes early in July
and on the road there are minas warming
their bare feet, savouring as cars
approach the small dangers of delay,
then cavorting upwards into
a walnut tree to sit in its arms
and laugh, their white fingertips winking;
thin brown magnolia of the winter
briefly flowering before the dark.
They are like lovers who meet first when
they are old: impatient, selective, and moved
continually by an absurd delight.

The Party

For Keith and Jacqui

Although it is not yet September
sunlight lies along the leaves
about the open door; the room

is lit by laughter. Women move
in coloured skirts, long and sleek,
the wine is high in glasses, but
there is no music: we have too much
to say – we were a generation
committed to total elucidation.

This stout sociologist
just back from sabbatical
you notice does not listen well,
but through his restless glance looks still
the fiery youth who yelled at crowds
one Anzac Day, years before
the protest marchers came, defaced
the cenotaph, went to gaol
for a fierce, pacific creed
in 1939.

This delicate woman, very French,
and beautiful like all Americans –
silver eyelids, pale crisp hair –
she's on vacation from Toronto,
in her purring vowels talks well
about McLuhan whom she's heard
making epigrams; knows
him for a prophet. She has read
everything . . . her pearly smile
serves, but not for amusement.
She was a nervous, clever girl
trying to belong with those
she never quite knew well enough
Merci mille fois Madame

I remember . . . yes, do you . . . ?
I never took him seriously;
this considering, gentle man
talks now about – talk.
The shifts and codes of language have
made shape and sense of all his old
uneven ideologies.
He married late, and happily;
his son, a shy boy, is here.

The fading sunlight falls on tall
white grasses, queerly still
against the crimson wall.
Few of us are under fifty;
my dear and loving friends I raise
my glass. The party's done. I think
that you will never come again.

At Pyes Pa

My father, a mild and unheroic man,
died bravely; shrunken by disease
and disappointment he lay on the verandah
he had built, seeing across his partly
planted orchard a blue shimmer of sea
and mountain in a country rich, he had
supposed, in continuity. Smiling
at us he comforted his children: death
was not so great a thing that we should fear it;
he could for instance visit us in dreams . . .
His hands, brown as earth, lay on the bed;
we were to care for his trees. We cried
but could not speak – what comfort could we offer,
who felt our good health like an accusation?

Katherine

I am shocked at your
mid summer
mid morning
mid adolescence
no-sense
judgment

36

things fade when exposed
to a harsh light too soon
before the colour is set
in poems or people
do not go
my child furred bud
green orange
not ripe yet for picking
bud-scent and blossom
still in your hair.

Putting her hair up told your great-grandmother
life was beginning – one year older
than you she carried the first of the twelve
children who buried her, tiny child-woman,
body devoured by its secret bleeding,
barely twenty years later;
all the years afterwards empty as air
that has lost its green leaves and bright oranges
after the tree is cut down.

Girl leave your hair down
brown curling round
the white wax of your skin
in the sun
in the morning
Katherine, stay home.

The Study of Geography, or History

and a gesture of opposition to George Steiner

At school I scribbled in the margin of my atlas –
not liking facts connected with production, weather,
population, soil, I chose instead to wander
in countries never mentioned: Babylon, Byzantium,
the Persian city still called Tyre, or Samarkand
(and peacocks strutting in courtyards of milk-white marble),

Carthage,
golden city buried deeper than the tombs of Pharaohs;
even Abyssinia where, I had been told,
men sliced their meat off rumps of rams still running
wild – the screams of those terrified creatures were louder
than any teacher's exhortations to 'attend'.

Tonight in a small white house, in the raw country I
have always lived in, I listen to a cultivated
European voice say in English that
men are guests upon the earth: 'man is a cruel
carnivore built to move forward . . . but the truth
may be extraneous to his needs . . . ' The truth? So used
it is a scientists' word. Once more I see the sun god,
god of death, the falcon and the jackal, brooding
over the Old Kingdom, and Doric tribes building
temples of stone when Pompeii was a country town.
Above me the starlit southern sky shines with a patient
attentive brilliance on the dreams of hopeful men.

The truth – what is it but the answer men in time may give
to questions asked by men? If the future of a dying
universe is told in gaseous explosions
amid uninhabitable rocks, then
here, in the silence of a summer night where
the small cottages lie asleep, and the strangely
transparent faces of the moon flowers are lit up in the garden,
I affirm my tenuous humanity. The lost
territories of Byzantium, this village here – these
hold all the future I can recognise; I am afraid
of a star spinning into darkness unseen by living
eyes; or the truth that knows no voice to say its name.

Marigolds

for Virginia

African marigolds in a cold summer,
scraping with their brown fiddles a cheerful
scherzo until, far off, beyond the trees

and the grey southern water, they dance for us,
the small warm-bodied women, their black feet
stirring patterns in the soft-as-summer dust
in a tiny market place while the immense skies
of Africa blaze above them.

Here, unseasonable January gales
have blown across the hill path near my house
a full-grown pohutukawa, in flower
a month ago; now the green knobs
that held its seeds like fists, defiantly,
have turned aside as though to hide the secret
alterations of decay; the leaves
like women hang their heads and weep.

Summer, season of storms . . . until this year
I had not thought so; yet I know the marigolds
sing of other things – their message is also
of raiding parties in the hills, of eyes
half closed on moving targets beyond the mounded
red earth where border stations lie concealed.

Watched by the marigolds' bronze unblinking faces
tenderly I remove the dead bodies of the leaves.

Wintersweet

There is so little time for us
such a short savouring, such lightness
and elusiveness to our leisure – come quickly
give me your hand; if we walk too late
in this swiftly-chilling air
the frost will be upon us and every tendril
touched, blackened.

Who speaks of the slowness of age?

The winter rose, green frailty, is
a shaped shell, ear for the distant
green sounds of summer – cut, see how
it droops at once, folding limp hands
over its head, relinquishing all
its crispness without objection;
here, hooded by its green canopy,
it is safe for a day. Till the dark comes
leave it, leave it to its fragile dream.

Dear Uncle Harry

His house is furnished now with costly
ugliness; his wife complains,
he smokes incessantly
and does not know at all
why he should make her plead for money.

But I remember the scrubbed kitchen
table, the iron rain and far off a black
stick-figure bringing the sheep down
the pinched spurs; starlings scribbling
their mocking messages across the sky;

cousins Alice and Dorrie, shy
in my bedroom, veiled and tremulous
brides of Christ
distracted by conscience or command
from the cabbage-patch indignities
of home. Not for him – he was around the ewes,
stubborn profile against the winter
sky and a hard shine in eyes as blue
as the bleak Kaimanawas that sent him
storms to grip the skinny homestead
by the throat and shake it.

Summer and winter he grumbled up
the hills, topdressing by hand
(when he had a bag of super) coming in
to slices of mutton, dripping, bitter tea;
and the stars out, grinning over the paddocks.

Uncle Harry, burning off up the back,
what ambitions burnt you to the bone,
what rages shimmered between you
and the long blue afternoon? Who
could love you? Such luxury
upon such meagre means?

The land you fought your futile
wars against now flourishes
without you; you sit in ornamental chairs
and stare, not remembering how
failure found in you a fierce resolve.
Dear Uncle Harry, there are no rewards;
it is our dreams that destroy us.

Cicadas

The cicadas' chirping is everywhere,
it is a season's singing, the noisy
punch-drunkenness of existence – and
there they are, nearly an inch long
black thrusts of energy perched
on a lamp post, or in thousands filling
the trees with their madness; the world hangs
close – I can reach out and touch
its lovely dangerous
quickly-ripening skin before
the rough winds of winter sweep us away.

I hear you breathe sharply and laugh, see you
burn the blue light that snaps in your eyes
then turn softly towards me; it is this

that you want, you too, this great apple
tasting of time and corruption, warm flesh
full of sweetness presaging decay . . .
so fierce, so ordinary, our desire –
the cicadas sing of it, loud and exultant,
through a short season.

Six Poplar Trees

My death is close, it is here in the next room
talking quietly, waiting its turn for visiting
hour; they smooth my bed in readiness.

This is a reminder, an afternoon call
from an acquaintance who has remembered to bring
something I had neglected or forgotten.

What was it? Perhaps the six poplar trees over the river
standing still, sombrely pondering in the wind
that shakes the hospital garden, its roses and sunflowers;

or the inescapably clogging kindnesses
of nurses and cleaners, protecting us, stopping our breathing
with softest earth, closing our eyes with sleep . . .

This worm of blood that creeps into my arm
I scarcely feel; is it to nourish or
to devour? Does it come now or later?

Wellington Letter

I

Five o'clock; the winter morning's
no more than a bleak frontier
of the night. This rough hill, where
houses tilt to the tides of the rowdy
dark, gives just a hand-hold; we're
tossed among squally showers 'moderate
swell to the west, wind 20 to 30 knots'
– the marine forecaster's voice brings
a map of rainy seas, Kapiti to Cape
Palliser, Cape Palliser to Puysegur
Point, visibility 4 knots (from Stephens
Island to Jackson Bay the seas are
slight). And Nugget Point? He burrs,
knobbed as a knotted rope, a chunk
of cliff chops into the misty vision
slapped by a moderate southerly swell.
We rock into the windy morning. Yesterday
Evans Bay was a city of slim white ships.
I thought of you. Voices. Voices.

II

You are the smiling photo beside
the telephone, the laughter stilled
on a tape casually recorded. There are
other exact presences; it's true death's

winter passes, we meet in a new spring
and I walk your green aisles of silence
in a remembered confiding. In four years
I have given up straining, have learned
to stand still, unprotesting as forlorn
couples do when the train's gone, taking
a child to the dangerous city. Through
breaking clouds I see there was a true
madness in you – 'I'll eat a lily' only
you could say, and laugh, and do it
despite expostulations; poisonous?
You didn't care, taking yourself too
lightly even then. Four years. It's
hardly time, yet this is the work
grief gives, to set about composing
the lifetime that we thought we knew,
without falsity or fear to try to make
it whole. One remains accountable.

Death's an explosion in the mine
of love; this letter tells of
reconstruction, failed attempts,
of gifts, of visitations from those
who come like neighbours bringing
soup and clothes to families made
homeless by disaster; so love
returns, limps in, is recognised.

III

Thomas Hardy leaned
against the trunk
of an oak and said
with the deep-reaching
whimsy of the man
of earth and education
'This tree is
a man I knew'.

                    Ten
feet down the bank
where last year's
storm has gouged
a niche of clay
I planted a totara
for you, its tough
sprigs to contain
your delicacy,
your grace, Rachel.

IV

Let us consider the poet
as fool, a patient undignified
creature, poor at self-protection
– Joyce for instance, disgraceful
in the importunity of his love,
writing beseeching letters to Nora
who hardly knew how to contain
his excessiveness . . . Sappho
of the violet braids declaring
the hurt and childlike heart;
Tsvetayeva, tremulous extravagant
woman, walking about the dusky
Kremlin sleepless with indignation
at every fresh suffering,
crying out her compassion
to the sound of Moscow bells.

My story is of a room haunted
by the cold light of July, and
in the morning mail a small
orange-covered book, Rilke's
requiem for his young poet – 'you
gladly, you passionately dead' –
of his questioning, was it *this* . . .
did you not feel some warmth,

like a firelit room, as you slipped
out? Did you know of the moment
to come, and you not to be there?

He was my voice in the silent
morning, he burnt my timid evasions
as a fire in the slums destroys
and cleanses; he took me outside
to breathe the biting air. This was
the new seed that forces aside the dried
stalks of the wasted bracken; he stood
his ground. We recognise the great
poets by their unshakeable courage.

V

One life's a small thing,
you'd have said, a servant
who waits and carries, one
who passing pauses to perform
trifling useful acts;

the young girl, it may be,
who brings fresh bread,
tomatoes, beer, and spreads
a cloth beneath the willows
in a corner of the scorching
hay field.
                    Just so you
folded up the years, like
a cloth to leave beside
the basket in a cooling
kitchen – and the starlings
blowing like a shower across
the summer sky;

                    then
slipped outside and darkness
came in with its tranquil
disregard.
             I hear you
saying 'nothing was ever
mine'. We learn, we borrow;
none completes the task.

VI

I heard news today
of the men who search
the earth for lost
lives, finding in each
marked stone or ring,
broken potsherd,
scrap of painted clay
or rusted blade
the mute whisperings
of the same tale
we, momentously
it seems, can tell
out loud. They found
in Germany a tomb
of Celtic origin
in which some royal dream
of immortality
had placed a four-wheeled
chariot decorated
with flying horses, gold
inlaid; near it a narrow
coffin, boat-shaped for
the timeless journey
to *Tir inna mBeo*.
In old Bohemia
the most corrupt prince
could there retrieve
his primeval innocence.

VII

I remember a small room and the sounds
of morning tiptoe-ing discreetly
by – a rooster's faint falling cry,
the milkman's pony pock-pocketing along
the street, a sparrow's phrase or two;
myself drowsing on a stool, one bundle
with my milky baby, united in the
creased-silk enclosing clasp of mouth
and breast, the same slow vibration
stirring both absorbed bodies – a
perfection of giving and receiving,
yet it was not anything achieved;
the art was just to let it happen.

VIII

'Let's discover pub talk' the young poet
pronounced, 'not to set ourselves apart . . .'
Well, it was all there, the carpet thick
with beer, the juke box hollering, a little
joker no one knew coming and going with
the mild and muddied bonhomie of booze –
a good fellow without doubt but I think,
poet, he doesn't want to be romanticised.

Yet I admit we proved some point about
the place, four of us attending to those
two – good men, respectful, never close
till now – while they told tales of work
and friends, theories, mistakes and
passionate misconceptions; a touch solemn
(that was the beer), certainly excessive;
it was a subtle, risky sharing, abandoned

yet more watchful than it looked. Listening
I thought of old and common voices; was it
thus, perhaps, the dialogue that asked
around for truth (the elusive comrade)
while laurel sticks were doodling in
the hot Athenian dust?

      Then they embraced,
laughing crazily, and you could see that
every one of us was drunk with love.

IX

I read his words, he mine
– an entertainer's gesture
you say, or poet's posture,
this tossing a borrowed line;

if so, it was a surprise
that the word is quick, a creature
faithful to its nature
yet cunning in disguise:

your poem's a bird that flew
into my leafy places,
its white sheen graces
a green obscurity.

My voice was careful, quiet:
so to stalk a stranger
I felt the mystery, the danger;
breath took its shape from the heart.

Poet, say, do you know
you now perpetually
will carry a chirrup of me
and I a whistle of you?

X

Whoever loves may hurt
simply, without cruelty,
as a swimmer
clasps another
in the iridescent glimmer
of the summer water
and coils and turns, the light
shining like scales along
their liquid bodies,
then drops his arms
to cross the slippery
pool alone, as the cold
current comes.

XI

There are fixed points
like stars; they wake each night
after days of flux and we say
'this is love'. It is not so easy –
to hold your frail poise
you must stand against me;
when the lout comes in to the room
you must leave and speak to him.

This shaggy brute must follow us
into the moonlight where we walk
distracted under the jagged galaxies.
On the icy grass by the precipice
it will be his selfish insistence
that mortifies and saves us.

XII

Across the moonlit bay low roofs
hunch in the hills; on this side
the legal town – white walls, terraces,
the luminous spray of cherry trees
in bloom, the spring night strolling
among swept paths, weeded corners,
fresh turned earth.

                    There, it's
institution polish, whiff of a late
illicit smoke, footsteps, keys,
the sharp rejoinder of the lock.

In the Day Room we chatted painfully,
trying to breathe life into memories
and messages; he walked in jerks, stubbed
out ten cigarettes in half an hour.
Someone's girl cried endlessly. Leaving
I looked back; he stood in his too-tight
denims, handsome, tarnished, a tall
cup drained and set aside.

                    See how the moon
glitters on the water, see it flash knives
upon the quivering water, see it search
the dark like torches in an alley way; how
it creeps and turns and blows its whistle;
oh with what brute impartiality it
lights up the million miles that lie
tonight between my friend and me.

XIII

For Pablo Neruda

Poet who travelled every country
except mine, who never saw these
formal ferns uncurl among last year's

brown stalks and the spring light dart
over this rapid southern river; nor
smelt the grass, sun-spiced already
in the tingling valley; poet with
the black eyes and cracked fingernails,
singer who went swinging the red bells
of your dream to bring your song
to the people, and your sadness for
those imprisoned 'in walls of their
own making' . . . I hear you, even
here, louder than the cries of children
playing in the river shallows, fresher
than the new-gleaming rye grass; your
strong heart touches mine, as for a moment
bare arms brush, in a crowd which has
unknowingly jostled them together.

XIV

More and more she cries, at two years
old, and more again – more plums more
trees more nests and eggs (and squawking
hens) more pips and melons dribbling
from more lips, more dancing on the roof
more night more day, sun splintering
through cracks of early morning doors,
more floors more bare feet curling on
their woody sheen, more arms and elbows
toes and breasts, more white and smooth
more round and small, more slips of
grassy tips and petal shine, more
gold and black and rosy, smell of feathers
warm, wet, more scrape of gravel, kiss
of dust, more soft sour sharp-sweet,
more shooting stars more midnights,
milk and apples, mountains, cats' miaows
and mornings – more, she says. And now.

XV

All this week
I was sick,
last month I suffered
constant headaches,
earlier I broke my arm
and it was slow to heal.
In time my children will die
and their children
and it will be as though
I had never lived;
but the earth will remain,
these delicate willows
touching the river water
will pass through perpetual summers
and women I shall not know
will walk among their trailing
scarves of silk, papery and green.

XVI

Let me tell you of my country, how it
suffers the equivocal glories, the lean
defeats of a discontented not a tragic
people; how it dreams in small townships
of interest rates and deals, possible
adulteries, the machinations of committees,
sickness and the humanely disguised
failures of children – not hunger, seldom
despair, but perhaps a rifle shot across
the dark paddocks, the indefensible sting
of a snub, the ache of boredom . . .

I tell you too of the tiny jewelled
orange trees of the north and the cloudy

vineyards, grape bloom mornings of summer
on Hawkes Bay hills and the noonday
shimmer, sky as blue as a bird's egg;
Gate of Haast and the sweep from earth
to heaven, the mind soaring ten thousand
feet in an instant; or the flame of the high
country tussock in August, the sky blue-
black and old Ruapehu hunching its
shoulders into a jacket of snow . . .

In this land of giant angularities
how we cultivate mind's middle distances;
tame and self-forgiving, how easily
we turn on one another, cold or brutish
towards the weak, the too superior . . .

As I write the morning still sleeps
on the white water – that same sea
that through ripe and oblivious seasons
must flare at last into horizons that
we have never learned to recognise

XVII

Every remark she makes is vague,
abstracted, and over and over
he can't prevent his hands from
stroking her lovely hair (though
in my sitting room he tries);
they touch the talk with finger
tips, passing in a paper arabesque,
profound, absorbed; from paper
glasses they drink the air.
Rapt somnambulists.

But where they really are
they blaze with light, gold leaf

suits encase them, head to toe . . .
I think suddenly of the gilded
cupid who died of his fancy
dress, every pore starved for air . . .
but no, worry's a cowardice, like
asking his aim in life, his weight
as a citizen, how he'll shrink
or swell in middle age. It's life
or death – and perhaps they don't
care which (it's the plausible
imitations they can't imagine).
Every question's vulgar.

Dazed, they rise from armchairs,
Adonis no taller nor Venus more
voluptuous, smile remotely,
move outside to ride the summer
afternoon in the pounding chariot
of lust and innocence. And I?

I wash and put away the painted cups
from which we drank ambrosia.

XVIII

Dear and gentle ghost, I have come
to an end; and did not find, as
perhaps I hoped, that you would speak
again if we could find the words.
Rather I know that though love's sick
body is restored by love there is none
great enough to cross the seas that roar
between our separate mountain tops.
We embark; there is no arriving.

You have your choice, I mine; and soon
we shall both be one with the constant

earth, the tides that put out to
the hurting uncertain future; strange
gods will brood above our sleep of
clay, their voices echo through us
where we lie, change, dissolve,
take on new lives. We are the cells
of time; snow will fall upon us
with its crisping touch, wind blow
our dust, water wash us in the pebbled
body of the sea, and the stars
take always their dark road.

Our words will be lost but our love
will enter the life of the land
like the dust a sunset lights up
with its recurring fire. Now the sky
broadens, sun touches the water.
I tell you it will be a fine day.

From *Seven*

A Meeting

Shy, you are air and fire,
I cannot touch you; in
the smoky shadows I glimpse
quick-running creatures
with eyes of apprehension
and delicate antlers held
away from the tangled
trees; the thud of feet
marks a secret rhythm.

I draw back, close the parted
branches. This is the place
where love or death may burn
the naked skin; in the dark wind
sound the poet's fearful voices.

Prague 1977

They behave, as we all do, according
to temperament. I dined with a gallant
gentleman, his words like the wine keeping
a clear and piquant flavour. The bitter
sediment he tastes alone – sleepless
at night perhaps, after bad news

of friends, or receiving a letter
containing irrelevant explanations
for cancelling his appointment.

Thinner, harsher of speech and jaw,
the poet talked of work; putting it
on the table he dissected it carefully –
we write you understand because we must –
his clean code would consider talk of
loneliness untidy, and probably unkind.

At gun point I would like to think
the temperament I became could dress,
put on its terror quietly and dine out
with such men, filling death's glass
with an unshaken courtesy.

Ghosts I

On summer nights
I dream of Africa.
A black man sleeps
on the earth and
beside him pass
the rough feet of children;
his body is curled
against the light,
he turns without waking
to the dry breast
of the land.
The sun falls blinded
out of a smoking sky.

Ghosts II

And after all a slave sits out the centuries
among her betters – a marble general, rows
of emperors – the little *inconnue* some
French committee bought, noticing perhaps
her pert and unpatrician nose, a ghostly
sparkle in eyes long blinded by their dust.

It is as though, unsuitable as ever, she still
slips out into a bustling Roman dusk to where
her lover waits beside his stolen clay, in
a grimy courtyard by the river; she's to sit,
he says, as long as there's a thread of light . . .
stupid! nights she knows are not for that –

and lifts her head and curses, ignorant
little slut; and he, breathless, fire to
his fingertips, catches her magnificence.

Back Street

A young man cold and shocked
mumbling before the policeman's brusque
demands; rain; an ambulance
that blocks the traffic,
through a banging door the wind
and comfortless passageways.
What pain, what crudity
in this poor place –
and I, driving past, considering
the fine silkiness of words
that may illuminate relationships.

Town and Country Matters

For A. C.

I have seen the sparrows gathering
at nightfall, thousands coming to perch
in two black pine trees in an asphalt corner
of the city; I have heard their screaming –
it's as though there's a victory for us all,
urban guerillas, coming out just then
from our cover . . . And I would exult too
– but are we not to carry files tomorrow,
and agree with the general secretary?
I will talk instead to you, dear friend;
sea birds rise over your hills, and when
you leave us it is their wild cry you hear.

From *Salt from the North*

A Note from Auckland

The almond tree is in flower
each blossom a star giving
out its pale and crystalline
radiance. Over the hill
the hospital is full of the hurt
of people holding tightly to
being alive, and some who must
drink the black juices of death.
I am shaken by it, as the wind
shakes these petals in the blue
rain of the sky. When you read
my letter some will have fallen
into the dark mould of the earth,
but you will know of this
flowering in a distant city.

Round Oriental Bay

This is my city, the hills and harbour water
I call home, the grey sky racing over headlands,
awkward narrow streets that stirred me long ago
– it's half a lifetime since I first came in
wonderment and savoured here prodigious
conversations, gravid with abstractions, in Mount
Street cemetery; read Eliot; acted plays that

occupied us night long – planning, having visions,
making love with all the light sweet leisure
of the young till startled by the dawn we walked
still softly laughing to our dingy old addresses,
returning later for the talking, always talking,
in the drowsy gorse on Varsity Hill.

What else? The shared penury, our monumentally
naïve political convictions; our cleverness
(the 'vicious little circle' marvelling at its
brilliance for a fragile funny summer term);
our simplicity – 'If you won't marry me
I'll wait for you for ever' – ah, it was all
for ever . . . and now what's left of it, that
passion so intense there was a kind of moral
splendour in it, those helpless loyalties?

The bell of Saint Gerard's booms gently in the dusk;
the city's strict oblongs of light are new,
but in these hills the past is soaked like blood
that soaks a battlefield; the restless water grinds
the pebbled beach, before the island's dark hump
opens the winking red eye of the buoy; above me
lights wake too in gabled houses – the battered,
windswept, hill-top houses that still stand
and face the constant beating of the weather.

To a Grandson

Citizenship: United States

Child, behind your eyes old memories sleep,
of journeys your father's people made
from Europe to the alluring continent,
of his still restless wandering over
Africa, that bitter beautiful land;

conceived there, you were born in a Bedu
hospital beside the sea in a country
once ravaged by the Persian kings.
Distance lives in you, a gypsy valour
awake to every perilous initiation.

Yet your blood is ours too, antipodean
inheritance from generations of hill-
country farmers – sheep men, shrewd,
salt-tongued, black-tempered, their horizon
the jagged line that cut a temperate sky;

the travels of these men were a few
days' ride, their landmarks loneliness,
a bad season, cranky wives; theirs too
a warring at the frontier of that elusive
summer country we all believe is home.

Morning in Christchurch

Through the singing of birds I rise
slowly from sleep; this garden, the city,
these islands have moved into morning;
over the sea that wraps the unreachable
curves of the earth, continents sleep.
It is dark in New York. Last night I read
that Robert Lowell is dead – and look
now towards that populous American night
wondering, puzzling . . . for it is not grief
we feel at a great man's death, but a kind
of apprehension, as though some piece
of a vivid pattern has dropped
from its place, and left a darkness
we know to be ours. I imagine the rooms,
the desks under lamps, the rough tables
where men and women will search with
judicious patience for a new light,
remembering the place where he gathered
his graveyards and grainy seas, his rooms
full of angular eccentric relations
and tortured heroes; his grim wisdom.

Greek Antiquities: First Floor

Little sculptured animals, young deer
still stiffly running, still with bright
and frightened eyes, my fingers touch
the tiny perforations that mark
the spots upon your coats of clay
and find them rough and hard. Will any
dream of mine so run, wakeful
through more than twenty centuries?

Three Women

Green the drawn curtains, the walls,
the very air is green where our
discovered words uncurl new tendrils.
Exile? Yes of course we talk of it,
meaning different things.

Yours, familiar, stands before
your house in full leaf; through it
you glimpse chimney pots and spires.
My startled reappraisals struggle,
needing time to root and grow.

The lamplight's clear pool gravely
reflects our difference, our likeness.
You pour Dutch gin from a terra cotta
jar; we speak of home as children
there might speak of England.

Morning light is harsher; in the early
train a woman sits rigid, her whole
body clenched yet helpless to hold
the tears that cover her face . . .
black, among the English newspapers.

Town Ghost

After the rain
came the town ghost
eyes like street lamps
yellow sulphurous
fists big boulders
coat black in the wind
strode past the wharves
round into Cable Street
shoved aside spectres
warehouse porters
flower auctioneers
aching with injury
silently bawling
when I came up
spat on the asphalt
Look lady just don't
you interfere.

Sonnet for the Unsung

At his death she came for the first time
to the house; along the panelled hall
with other mourners she moved beneath the pall
of general grief and had her place; no name
was given. But when she came to where he lay
among the piled lilacs, and at once saw
that familiar precious habitation now
even from her sealed, locked away,
she turned aside and, bracing her mind
to take alone the weight of what they'd kept
together in a delicate poise to the end,
she walked through crowds staring at where he'd slept
into the garden his sons had helped him tend
and sat alone and bowed her head and wept.

The Distaff Line

So late your letter comes – forty years
and now this wild face, round-eyed child
crossing the dark field of consciousness
and closer, suddenly old, holding me with
a fierce mnemonic stare. How shall I learn
a lifetime in an instant? Turn back, we'll
go together down a lengthening road, find
the orchard, the track of spongy elephant
grass that leads to the apricot tree.

Look, here's the raffish village, here
the ha'penny store, the bar hump-backed
like a whale that crammed with mud the green
throat of the river; and here the trees,
apples, pears, spindly plums, last and best
the apricot, grey grandfather drowsing
in a dusty light. Now see a familiar shadow
fall upon the grass as those formidable
women – your mother, midwife to a hundred
Maori families, mine their children's
teacher – country women, tall as scarecrows,
arrive to summon us to evening rituals
ordered by their brisk instruction.

Old friend, cousin, let us say the secret
creatures behind our eyes have not grown
old (and were they ever young?) – come,
lay your cheek against the green skin
of the river, grasp the branch that
holds the ripest fruit, we'll sit here
as we did before through endless amber
afternoons of childhood's summer.

But there's your letter – which I shall not
answer, guessing your reticences well enough.
It shows you, as I would have thought,
straight-backed and calm, a little stately,
looking Master Death severely in the eye,

never doubting that the only failure is
a loss of nerve. So it's to be. The ripeness
now has fallen from the trees and in the dusk
your face puts on its mask, rubric of
a resolute clan whose women's voices,
unshaken, ever spoke the word that called
us in and put an end to all our playing.

The Frontier

From the station at Garavan,
tiny platform squeezed against
the rocky Ligurian Alps, you can
walk to the Riviera; passing
tourists exhausted by leisure
and gazing at that relentlessly
picturesque sea, in ten minutes
you come into Italy.

On a cold sunlit morning I bought
from the frontier station a map
of Europe; each name spoke its own
language – München, Praha in the Czech
lands, Roma, Firenze, Genève; most
foreign to me was in this most true,
most deeply, securely itself. In
the glittering Mediterranean
light I climbed the rough road to
the mountains; there Roman villages
lie sealed fast against all tongues,
the faithful, the ignorant.

The Beech Tree

It's over, the rending shudder,
the crack; the tree's despatched –
and with it the long-settled

communities of green gossiping,
rapt occupations of birds,
the shared calamities of weather.
We crowd beside the stump, watch
sap like a kind of bleeding ooze
out of the packed encircling
substance of the wood; this
morning's act exposed
a century's patterned industry,
the years' circumferences
gathered cell by inching cell
out of the inner and the outer
lives of growth and weather.

And I think how in us too such
cycles move, how silently our accidents
and errors, the slowly multiplying
comprehension of our loss, our joy,
accumulate till every season of
the heart's engrained within us.

I tell you, friend or lover, all
who touch my life, I cannot lose you
even by forgetting until death destroys
the ordered secret kingdom of my body.

After Chagall

'Intensity and detachment: court both.'

The streets of my city grow old and small,
they are turning into a Russian village;
great waves of indigo light carry me up
and up into a populous sky; I attenuate,
turn upside down and float, the air streams
past billowing like iris blue chiffon, I
come to you on a house top where you are
playing on a red guitar the old songs

of the people; stars dance in the angle
of your elbow; we touch and our bodies
merge in a moving cloud of light turning
to paradisal green. There is no sound
but the hum of our hearts. The painter
is right, the real world could never
contain us. This is intensity.

Now the air thickens, the radiant company
darkens – bodies, birds, cows, violins and
harvest moons come drifting down, they
coalesce; we blink and look again at men
in suits smoking and talking of the news
in the morning paper; women's heads
repose on shoulders, mouths talk and eat,
bodies merely breathe. I struggle, choking
on the denseness of the air, look everywhere
but cannot find you. When it no longer hurts
to stand still and fit into the strict shape
of my skin – that will be detachment.

First Journey

In the warm dark I am alert
with wakefulness, watching where
new fears crouch ready to spring;
lights across the harbour mark with
an alien glitter the sea's metallic
mirror. At my window I see through
that other glass your turning away,
all farewells over, and the uncountable
miles taking their first slow
steps inexorably between us.

Now you are riding the eerie roads
of the sky, sitting, eating remarkable
food, smiling perhaps at a poised

freshness that begins to dance
for you upon the crabbed old planet's
edges. My last, my youngest daughter,
companion of the warm domestic years,
is it possible – can the earth so
split wide and fling you across
its scattered precarious frontiers?

I shiver; for it is something more
than distance that exacts silence
from the tender guardians of home,
when the young neophyte goes trembling
to her first mysterious lesson. I shall
not know if when snow falls in Europe
it is the ache of exile hurts you,
as you stand in a street of strangers
and touch for the first time
those cold and spiny crystals.

Learning to Ride

Remember the sunlight tumbling
among willows, the creaking of
saddles, the dust? – and round
the paddock, jolting and bouncing,
the child, a brown knot tied, too
loose, on the nag's enormous shoulders?
– the hands' fierce holding, the whole
small stubborn body shouting
determination not to fall . . .

It's a speaking body still, each
impulse defined in arch of bone or
pliant web of skin; see her twenty
years later wrenched by grief, head
bent to listen, arms to comfort
a helpless company; the hands that
mimed a child's resolve learn now

the solemn language of compassion.
Love in her is a steadiness of line,
a concentration in the eyes,
an angle, a spring held in the
flesh's taut dialectic.

Dear girl, when you ride again
let it be over round hills,
the cliffs not too close, let
your hands lie easily now
and under green willows
catkins fall on your hair.

A Difficult Adjustment

It takes time, and there are setbacks;
on Monday, now, you were all ennui
and malice; but this morning I am
pleased with my handiwork: your
stick figure moves, your two eyes
are large and dark enough, your
expression is conveniently mild.
You have begun to disagree with me,
but weakly, so that I can easily prove
you wrong. In fact you are entirely
satisfactory.
              I suppose, really, you are
dead. But someone silently lies down
with me at night and shows a soothing
tenderness. I have killed the pain
of bone and flesh; I suffer no laughter
now, nor hear the sound of troubled
voices speaking in the dark.

Latter Day Lysistrata

It is late in the day of the world
and the evening paper tells of developed
ways of dying; five years ago we would not
have believed it. Now I sit on the grass
in fading afternoon light crumpling pages
and guessing at limits of shock, the point
of repudiation; my woman's mind, taught
to sustain, to support, staggers at this
vast reversal. I can think only of
the little plump finches that come
trustingly into the garden, moving
to mysterious rhythms of seeds and
seasons; I have no way to conceive
the dark maelstrom where men may spin
in savage currents of power – is it
power? – and turn to stone, to steel,
no longer able to hear such small throats'
hopeful chirping nor see these tiny
domestic posturings, the pert shivering
of feathers. They know only the fire
in the mind that carries them down
and down in a wild and wrathful wind.

I do not know how else
the dream of any man on earth can be
'destroy all life, leaving
buildings whole . . .'

Let us weep for these men, for
ourselves, let us cry out as they bend
over their illustrious equations; let us
tell them the cruel truth of bodies,
skin's velvet bloom, the scarlet of
bleeding. Let us show them the vulnerable
earth, the transparent light that slips
through slender birches falling over
small birds that sense in the miniscule
threads of their veins the pulses of

every creature – let these men breathe
the green fragrance of the leaves, here
in this gentle darkness let them convince me,
here explain their preposterous imaginings.

Reading a Poem by Elizabeth Jennings

Yes you must stay away,
I say fiercely, sitting with a book
and practising solitude;

I even toss my head, lose
the place – but it slipped
anyway, pages earlier.
My heart hurts with holding on.

But how well it is working –
my blood is as cold as an otter's
and the words are clear; they say
'in Eden, or oblivion'.

They are ice frosted on a window
shining delicately. I touch
the glass – 'oblivion' – but my mind
is clumsy with cold. 'Eden' – it begins
again, struggling to trace the precise
unexpected threadings;

now they spread a little,
blurring like grey flakes that
fall on my hands, they melt
and run down. I am alone
and you will not come.

Applied Astronomy

For Ruth

To answer the question posed by Mr Hoyle
– was there one big bang or does creation
endlessly continue – I need not peer
among the midnight-shadowed stars; this tiny
creature proves both theories tenable.
Her beginning was the still moment
in a moving tide, dark beyond all
discovery; spinning atoms caught into
a new grain of life; soundless explosion.
Yet almost everything is still to come.

Black-haired scrap of frowning dim
absorption, your wide eyes wander still
in cloudy space beyond the earth, strange
shore on which you find yourself washed up
by storms whose source you cannot guess.

But your struggle has begun; from this
hot and troubled little head the smell
of crying comes; we are inordinately
grateful when you smile. You are the surety
we need that shocks of birth and death are
big bangs only and in between, creation's
widening circles may carry us perhaps
beyond the farthest stars. Small girl,
dearly loved, you have picked up your life.
I wish you strong and easy holding of it.

Another Christmas Morning

In the dark hall a pine tree, small, absurd
and bravely lit, sheds like incense the smell
of old and passionate surprises – a furred
bear, tight-held in tears, a book, a doll . . .
I close the door and step into the early

summer morning, hushed above me, high
and still as a cathedral. Here patiently
the ancient gods anoint the earth, cry
blessings on the season; birds' madrigal
sings the passing of the bitter days;
from every death this summer festival
brings green beginnings; no grief endures.
Now sleepers awake, the warm house draws me in
– quotidian cloister where love is born again.

Incident

Your eyes were shiny black as melon
seeds; it was your birthday. Even so
your father, busy, raged when interrupted;
tears on your hot small face, you stood
beside me as he opened letters, read
aloud a friend's poem: the new Vietnam
war, a village massacre, the deaths
of children . . . the sunlit Saturday
morning room was still, you clutched
my skirt; woman, child, we peered at him
together from a difficult silence.

And I thought of Brendan Behan's
drunken compassion – wild rapscallion
Dubliner, but wise: 'when we weep,'
he said, 'it's always for ourselves.'
How else I ask you, poets, fathers,
are we to learn of violence? Or of love?

Love Poem

Everything will happen. Your friend
will go to Paris, my uncle give up

at last his dreams of wild horses
flying over the hills of his boyhood
farm; that quaking marriage will break.

We do not speak of ourselves, but as
we walk down the stairs snow falls,
coming to lay soft stars on the dark
tweed of our hearts. We brush away for
each other the little messages of death.

In the street there are two young men
exuberantly quarrelling; we pass slowly,
close together and carefully keeping
in step. It is as though we have
something very light and fragile to carry.

Image for Stephanie

Above the cold and unquiet bay
glowers the cliff, a hundred feet
of crabbed acicular bushes –
matagouri, manuka, gorse, scrubby
things gritting their teeth for
the southerly's whipping as it strides
in from the Heads, swings its lash
round the northern hills and comes
down on these defiant crags.

Towards the top, bent a little towards
a protecting niche, stands a slight
tree starred with surprising flowers –
fragile, clustered together like small
faces; its name is *whau*, a local mulberry.
Slenderly poised, it hides a rare potency:
enclosed in white petals of virgin purity
every stamen's fertile. And through
deadliest weather the roots hold hard.

Street Scene

Each step is strange –
not simply difficult
but a kind of discovery
as though he arrived
surprised before some mist
had cleared. The yellow
jacket's 'town wear' but
he forgot the rest and
wears his slippers still;
in them he reaches forward
into each separate, minute
miracle. Is being old
like being very drunk –
each ordinary act
a triumph, hard-achieved?

Going to Nepal

For Clive

We think to learn possession by its practice
– a bicycle at Christmas, the lover's flowers,
the reassuring pacts of hospitality,
choice of vase or chair, precision
tools; but all the time – our children
could have told us – the intricate
homunculus was toiling with his clay
and leaves, frowning, dipping at
the marshy edge to give the raw earth
eyes and fingers, bangles from the fire
and voices spiralling upwards from
its painted mask, the worshippers agog.

Later however the oracle is less
convincing; a little bored, you leave
the over-decorated shrine and wander up
into the higher hills; there you see
how great rocks flow with natural waters,
wind and tussock sing their wild
and secret song, and each is nothing
but itself. You too. Now your heart
is bare. The earth that none may covet
comes to lay a hand upon your shoulder
and at last and modestly you speak
of it; the mountain is your brother.

The Names

Six o'clock, the morning still and
the moon up, cool profile of the night;
time small and flat as an envelope –
see, you slip out easily: do I know you?
Your names have still their old power,
they sing softly like voices across water.

Virginia Frances Martin Rachel Stephanie
Katherine – the sounds blend and chant
in some closed chamber of the ear, poised
in the early air before echoes formed.
Suddenly a door flies open, the music
breaks into a roar, it is everywhere;

now it's laughter and screaming, the crack
of a branch in the plum tree, the gasping
and blood on the ground; it is sea-surge
and summer, 'Watch me!' sucked under
the breakers; the hum of the lupins, through
sleepy popping of pods the saying of names.

78

And all the time the wind that creaked in
the black macrocarpas and whined in the wires
was waiting to sweep us away; my children who
were my blood and breathing I do not know you:
we are friends, we write often, there are
occasions, news from abroad. One of you is dead.

I do not listen fearfully for you in the night,
exasperating you with my concern,
I scarcely call this old habit love –
yet you have come to me this white morning,
and remind me that to name a child is brave,
or foolhardy; even now it shakes me.

The small opaque moon, wafer of light,
grows fainter and disappears; but
the names will never leave me, I hear
them calling like boatmen far over
the harbour at first light. They will sound
in the dreams of your children's children.

From *Catching it*

Moreporks in Menton

I have heard a morepork in Menton. Awake
last night, discovering in the disconsolate dark
how you need the shapes of the day to populate
the night (this cool French town says I must wait
for that), I heard its high quick call, those two
syllables of sorrow *No more! No more* –
yet it relents, and next time lets you know
it only asked you what you thought: *No more?*
No more? Poor bird, it belongs no more than I
– there are no owls along this coast; but above
us gods and heroes still wander in the olive
groves, Olympus itself is but a few
horizons east and in this heaven is set
great Orpheus, who may make music yet.
I am less a stranger for hearing the sly
and crafty Immortals in a morepork's cry.

Easter Saturday in Menton

The afternoon's still; spring rain falls
straight, drenching wild roses that hang
their heads over this cracked stone wall.
Last night the people carried the wooden
body of Jesus black-wrapped through
the streets of the old town, singing
in high sad voices as they've done
for a thousand years; today they hang

crimson silk on the pillars of Saint
Michel for Christ risen on Easter Day.

The rich tourists are left to the cafés
or to elbow about in the gift shops
shouting they don't speak the local lingo.
I too am a stranger, not less for knowing
I shall read my own name on a locked
letter box in the next lane. I remember
Easter as gathering mushrooms in wet
paddocks, piling raw logs on the hearth,
in the sting of the smoke lighting
the first fires on autumn evenings.

The road is deserted; there are a few
shut iron gates in the hedges, eddies
of mud, rubbish tins – and the roses.
Their scent is sharp in the rain.

Catching it

I saw three men looking
towards the sea:
they were on a seat, laughing –
three small brown foxy Frenchmen,
and the funniness of it
licking them over
like forked lightning.

In all of the ticking of time
it can never have happened before,

not like this, not exactly –
and the one by the sea wall
had a slack old jacket
done up with frogs
and a black fingernail
and a hole in the knee of his pants
– just to make sure.

Femme Agée

I was pretty once, I say it judiciously,
and he was mad for me, but I married my one
true love, my laughing companion; the other – he
went into the church. Now both are dead. Alone
I have to be the creature I've become –
the cruel jailer that was born in me and, since
it will not want to die, now takes my form.
I am disgusting to myself who once
was beautiful to them: that trembling jaw,
my clumsy step supported by a stick,
the veined old hand that grips it like a claw
– no man could so possess me, nor so mock.
Was this the pact my faithless body made?
Only a woman can be so betrayed.

The Ripening

The double-trumpeted datura
is said to be deadly. Out
of these waxen pendules
heavy with scent
and curled back at the edges
as though in derision
falls a dangerous dust;
drawn here
to the sun-cracked old seat
I'm advised not to fall asleep
under that stealthy rain.

The risk is keenest in spring.
For the late flowering
the sweetness is dulled;
so is the poison. But
by autumn we're all older,

when we go out our wisdom
walks with us –
or that rough cousin
self-regard.

Foreigner

The woman in the white dress
saunters past my gate
leaning against
the neat monsieur
buttoned into his French
alacrities.
They give no sign.

But I beside
the silent window
frowning
at my page
had waited for them;
with a precise casualness
I do not stare.

They are the frail wall
I lean against,
sunlit while summer lingers
and the purple bougainvillaea
blooms, luxuriantly native,
in the bright
conclusionless air.

In the Chemin Fleuri

I will remember today.
I know by its tingling –
the print on the skin of my back
of the iron fleur-de-lis of the fence,

the touch of the crabbed loquat branch
with its marbles of fruit,
against the white wall
the date palm's green tongues
whispering as usual and the grey dove
that comes every day strutting over the stones . . .

The very breath of the moment is flickering
here where I lean on the warm whorls
noting the first passionfruit flower
on the vine –
while all the time hearing
far off
the howl of the wind in the mountains
ice-black behind, if I look . . .

knowing that nothing is mine.

It's a spring morning,
it's a life, it's a shred I draw into the light
from that dark space where
nothing and no one belongs.
This is a day I'll remember.

One Way

Rain at evening; the ghostly outlines of rain;
in a foreign garden the shadow of places
I shall never come to again.

What an endless leaving our lives are,
how they stretch back complete with houses
and people, all directions familiar:

those we knew still yarning to one another
at doorways or in chairs out on the verandah
looking up at the weather

or in town at dusk hurrying to the bus stop
remembering near home to pick up a paper
and cigarettes from the last little shop –

'There!' we say, 'that was home,' and look
for ourselves in their faces; but there
is nothing. They don't want us back.

Perhaps we too have become, for them, the old town
now left behind for ever; and there is only
some strange garden, palm leaves; rain.

Jardin des Colombières

It's the country of childhood
authentic fairyland – walled garden
silent under cypresses
wild violets, primroses awake
in a delicate wood, stone bridge
spanning the legendary stream
marble pillars, dim heraldic halls.

I am the child of exiles who dreamt
of the lost garden. Here it is earth
and boundaries – it is property;
the eyes at the shapely window
are sharp with calculation. You pay
six francs to enter; the other, more
melancholy, cost I do not know.

Turning Point

All day I've been packing
and saying goodbye;
now I have just what I came with
– paper, a filled pen,
clothes for the journey.

85

The palm tree on the hill
turns and turns like a windmill
against the deepening sky
protesting that evening
has come too soon;

but further down the cypresses
are still, pointing as always
their dark fingers
and saying in shadowy voices
'Remember; remember.'

After Long Absence

My parachute floats down
veering slightly to right or left
in quivering currents
I am unmistakably approaching you
old friends
who look so like a small crowd
smiling and waving
anywhere
yet will confidently expect
the warm familiarity of flesh and blood
when inside my clothes
there is nothing
but the grey stone
of distant mountains.

Going to Moscow

The raspberries they gave us for dessert
were delicious, sharp-tasting and furry,
served in tiny white bowls; you spooned cream
on to mine explaining I'd find it sour.

The waitress with huge eyes and a tuft
of hair pinched like a kewpie so wanted
to please us she dropped two plates as
she swooped through the kitchen door.
No one could reassure her. Snow was falling;
when you spoke, across the narrow white
cloth I could scarcely hear for the distance
nor see you through floating drifts.

Then the tall aunt brought out her dog,
a small prickly sprig like a toy; we put on
our coats and in the doomed silence Chekhov
the old master nodded at us from the wings.
At the last my frozen lips would not
kiss you, I could do nothing but talk
to the terrible little dog: but you
stood still, your polished shoes swelling up
like farm boots. There are always some
who must stay in the country when others
are going to Moscow. Your eyes were
a dark lake bruised by the winter trees.

At the Museum of Modern Art

Paul Klee's particular inscriptions choose
the rare scale – opal flesh of fish, leaf camber,
crimson tubular shine on trumpet wall,

washed essence crystallizing tiny cubes
of afternoon, an elliptical smoke. He draws
each thread at the silvery hook's tip.

Beyond the straight hessian, more cilice
than curtain, steel claws six feet across gouge
the rocks and sludge that house New York;

the black hand on a knob teaches the blunt
beast a mammoth gentleness; thus it restrains
and places, thus elevates, divides; and thus

compels from the visionless ground a willed
mirage of columns and images. It is
by selection that we live and build.

To an Old Rebel

Feel how the round world rolls
in its rind of mountains and seas,
how we cling like flies to the morning
as we move from the shadowed arc of sleep
– oh Galileo, what adventuring that was,
what sternness, what gall, to push off
in your creaky reckonings from the level
earth into a nightmare of stars! Was it
heaven, though, phosphorescent through
the small telescope, or merely Jupiter's
moons? It's the question still; atoms
or Immanence, it curls an undying freshness
around our infections; the white fire
still draws us, and burns, and blinds.

At Delphi

No one knows how she was chosen, only
that she must have passed fifty, and when
the god called she would leave at once;
her children she might not speak to again.

Naturally she had come to think of them
with a certain mildness; on a hot morning
down in the Gulf see her gossiping to
her daughter as to another village wife –

though the girl's swollen belly is a shared
particular; almost equally they enjoy jeering
at the ribaldries of neighbours, their shrewd
peasant faces at such moments strikingly alike.

Is it a priest who arrives now, speaking in
a strange dialect – some tribe in the hills
more than likely – and launches into a queer
rhetoric to do with the power of sacrifice,

the all-pervading might of Apollo, telling
her softly that kings will come to her
where she sits high on the three-cornered
throne, to learn the god's inscrutable will . . .

But she knows only that the women have drawn
back, eyes peering round homely pillars are
suddenly secret with fear; that home has already
fallen away as surely as friends from a leper.

And this is the time: he leads her through
the hushed market place, the pregnant girl
alone and motionless by the well, her young
head haloed by the black Corinthian sun.

Climbing slowly in the heat to the shade
of a cypress, I have entered three thousand
years' silence; but the sacred Kastalian
spring is still the sound of a woman weeping.

The Garden Party

Yes I am here . . . and yours, if this
is what you want – this skin that fits
the insolent bone, the solemn fastidious

jaw, my broad-brimmed hat. There was
a moment when this cheek lay motionless
against the great side of the sea
quiet beyond the cries of rescuers:
I saw the end of that enduring blue
that rage, that discipline of blue –
and then they came. Now my drowned
darkness waits to take me home. I stand
among you, strangers angular as rocks,
and catch the last, the alien
light that shivers on the sand.

Word

'It is perfect' you say
and my pain listens
wearing its evil grin:
I grow faint
it leans over me
monitoring my defeat.
Wind cries at the corners
of winter streets.

' . . . because complete' you go on
with gentleness. I draw in,
flesh achieves
a new density.
I am a hurt cell
dark with life
that somewhere else
will elbow into joy.

The Readiness

It must have been there
like that pause before a clever line
so small it makes no space
to draw the ear; the cell of sound

where a first whirling
of the nucleus begins –

or perhaps it was a dry
transparent fragment, a seed
indistinguishable from
skeletal scraps of leaf or wood
as birth and death share
one visible patterning.

The chances are you saw later
the formed coils, ripe trees'
confusing shadows, an ugly scaliness
of bark, but not how these too
would grow. Now you must learn it
differently. Now it is your life.

Demande de Midi

I wait for you with a reluctant impatience
– it burns, this crucible of an arbitrary
desire; we do not need our youth to teach us
pain, who feel the cramp of habit, know
the slow shaping of the resistant grain.

And it is desperate enough, the act
by which we shall discover the accurate dark
that takes off one by one the customary
authorities of middle life; I fear
the body's cruelly meek discourtesy,

yet listen for your step as though
in the muted clamour of the dusk
there is no other; so eagerly shall I
expose perhaps to folly, cynicism
or neglect the long-protected years.

The evening draws aside to let you through,
I take your hand; like children, as defenceless
and as pure, we guard each other's hesitations.
And should we not so fear to penetrate
the blind and passionate reticence of age?

The Condition

Sun on our backs, we leaned on the wooden rail
and peered at the stream threading its beads of light
among the wavering stones; then we saw them, small
and resolute, two fluttering brown trout,
steady in the water, yet swimming manfully:
'If they go with the current they suffocate,' you said,
'a quick dash is sometimes possible, but only
by holding their breath, so to speak . . . ' Their need
is to engage the opposing current, to hold,
confront, defy, to judge exactly the weight
thrown each moment against their shoulders, their filled
and quivering gills. It's to know the force of the fight.
But I thought how they must sometimes long to turn and leap
uncaring into that swift and fatal sleep!

The Hedgehog

It rained in the afternoon
and I leaned out of the window, drawn
by the freshness of the garden
especially the marigolds
which are not sweet but resolute
even on dry days and I liked
their energetic and pungent
response to the rain.

So I leaned and looked, and wished
not to think of the room behind me
where my good friend
of the subtle intelligence
was gangling and twisting, possessed
by his disintegrating disease. Suddenly
there came in full daylight padding
the concrete path noiselessly in the rain
a hedgehog carrying its three-inch-long baby
in its mouth, and dropped it
beside the marigolds and went on
and came back
losing its way, forgetting the baby
which perhaps would die alone in the leaves
and went under a wall and was gone.

At last after a long wait
I turned back to the room
and the incoherently sick man and tried
to explain the calamity of the hedgehogs
and could not, for tears;
and the rain went on falling,
falling as though it would never end.

The Mountain

Oh love let us learn our love
now there is no more laughing in it –
let us remember the mountain
when we woke to the frost
and ran with our clothes to the kitchen,
airless and smelling of coal dust,
and dressed quickly in front of
the banked-up stove
glancing out at the glacier
gleaming on Girdlestone's shoulder . . .

and at night, how we stood
on the tiny porch together
and shook in the mazarine dark
and gasped and went in
shutting the door on the cold
and the mountain's terrible closeness.

Signs

The pronoun is
a tiny instrument we use
to unpick our lives; so 'I'
and 'you' begin to show
beneath the old shared knots
of 'us', so 'ours' is spoilt for 'mine'.
We do not know the dreadful pleasure
of our industry until
the rag's too weak to take
the weight of joy or compromise,
the pull and tear of love.

Red Nightgown

for Stephanie

I lie still, hardly breathing,
I must certainly not laugh or
she will wake, and we have had
enough of that for one night . . .
why else are we here in this
absurd nesting of mothers
and daughters? – I in my black

nightgown, curled round your
smaller blue, you round that
morsel in red, unfledged little
dreamer soaring in sleep
across adventuring heavens,
sure beyond all surmise
that tired and fallible women
will wait for her awaking.

Christmas as Usual

Nothing was unexpected –
the mother joyfully anxious
the child pure child
leaping for the luxurious tingling,
all surprises contrived
and truly enacted; one had come
four hundred miles, another
never leaves home. The fairy
at the top of the tree
is a rag of yellowing organdie
parcels are not now those
lumpy lettuce-leaf plates
nor samplers cobbled up into
oven cloths no one can use;
we have also grown out of the tears
and afternoon accusations
of the middle years –

but there's more news of deaths
and illnesses now, each year
they come closer; lazy, we lean
among shiny wreckage of paper,
possessions, the striped shirt
one sister made for another
the child's wonky LOVE FROM . . .

This is our ordinariness – and look,
we have learned it at last. Perhaps
it was always there waiting for us,
slightly childish; infinite. Mortal.

The Killing

Oh love's persistent,
won't give up its hold;
dismissed, creeps back
to tap all night at
sleeping windows; silenced,
maunders on – laughs too,
even here in the stained
dust to show how this
poor hen, grotesquely
on its feet, running as
it bleeds, still pursues
that old life of dirt
and sunshine our tomahawk
has shortly said is gone.

Ruth's Drawing

Four years old, you are
flying placidly
before a historic sun
– its yellow spikes command
a cosmic eloquence;

you passed without surprise
a purple jungle
now you leave the house top
rising plump and light
towards the top of the page –

there out of sight we stand
on level ground, feet astride
and breathing heavily;
we are busy exercising
our atrophied wings.

The Room

It came to this –
at evening you stood always
in the same place
frowning beside a shelf of books
that in your sullen calm you never
read. The strident silences between us
quarrelled without relief.

Tonight I come in to a listless
tidiness. For six months now the shadow
of your shadow's gone. The days curl up
and slumber undisturbed;
books are still unread, the quiet
vacated like a bus stop after hours.

Alone in this unbruising dusk
I ponder the bright and ready commotion
we for twenty years
reliably called home.

At the Gate of Number 89

Old woman among marigolds, her body
a sack of years propped up for the fall
of the saffron stars of the spring:
see how she moves and breathes with

the street, sags only by the hidden
unravelling of time as weatherboards
dry and weaken, doors crease and lean
a cobwebbed wall browns in the sun.

And there's the child who passes each day
and stirs with her bare feet the same
gravel patch for its pleasant scratching;
it's there now, she'll feel it for
seventy years, hear the old voice warming
itself at the usual fire – 'Lovely . . .
such bright cheeks . . . ' – though last night
both woke to the roar of motor bikes
up from the town, a man's body was
whipped and left in the stained
gutter, while they turned again to sleep
and a black wind howled from the dawn.

I think a city's spirit is always a woman,
long tried, grown old in the rain and rust,
the brawling winds of the street, knowing
that all that's alive can be bruised
and flung like a dog to the dark; but that
each morning, scuffing the dirty pathways
of being, comes again the indestructible
new born thing – shaft of sun, slummocky
floral dress, the child who will take
and keep for the term of a natural
life this mild equivocal blessing.

The Deal

Slashing honeysuckle on the hill
I breathe the metaphor
poets love gardens for – and it is true
this ruthless growth will smother
every other green thing,

and yet it binds us –
man woman house tree –
without it the caught ground falls
to the pit of clay below.

The sun mounts and holds me down.
Between earth and sky
I am fighting for my life.

The Quiet Populations

Let me tell you of my cat,
modest, intimate, complete,
my little cat that's dead.
Not of her suffering
though she cried almost
like a child at the end –
and it was a bloody death,
her bowels ravaged by a poison
someone meant for rats;
nor of my grief, but simply
of her creature presence,
her perservering like
a patient housekeeper
whose duties lie in keeping
fresh the plain habitual
furniture of living;

of the watching, nestling,
divining of moods, that
absolute compliance we take
from our animals as casually
as sun on summer days.
Secured by instinct from
perversities of change,
she kept with simple things
that move like quiet populations
through our lives – Vanessa,

sleek, black, green-eyed,
my delicate companion. A friend
buried her beneath the cherry
tree; it's budding early
– a salutation.

Crossing the Rimutakas

My wheels steady
the tilting hills.
Beside me sits
this happiness
looking about
and speaking with
a soft breathlessness.
It is very delicate,
too slight for all
I shall ask it
to bear. But look,
the early sun raises
its trombone above
the dark ridge
eight starlings
on a fence top
nod and wave as we pass.
Is it true what they say
– I shall need nothing
except my weakness
my transparency?

Those Roses

Roses, the single scarlet sort,
open at the throat as if for
coolness, sprawl at the window;

100

you heap on my plate a pile
of potatoes, steaming and small,
smelling of mint. 'They're
basic,' you say as we go at them
lustfully, 'they grow by the door;
you have to chase meat' – and I
notice a certain vegetable poise,
not striated like the fibrous
deposits of a more strenuous growing
but smooth, opaque; placid testimony
to the sufficiency of flesh.

'Of course you do have to hunt – '
I say, thinking of hopeful
burrowings in the soil, wresting
from the clutch of its black fingernails
each creamy nugget; and we agree
on that; we're a bit languid,
munching more slowly as each
pale pod splits open and fills
us with amber warmth – one flesh
sturdily giving itself to another.
Those roses, too, they lean over us,
and the squat black pot gives
off its dull gleam, grinning
crookedly from the stove.

New Poems

Epiphany

for Bruce Mason

I saw a woman singing in a car
opening her mouth as wide as the sky,
cigarette burning down in her hand
– even the lights didn't interrupt her
though that's how I know the car
was high-toned cream, and sleek:
it is harder for a rich woman . . .

Of course the world went on
fucking itself up just the same –
and I hate the very idea of stabbing at
poems as though they are flatfish,
but how can you ignore a perfect lyric
in a navy blue blouse, carolling away
as though it's got two minutes
out of the whole of eternity, just
to the corner of Wakefield Street –

which after all is a very long life
for pure ecstasy to be given.

Camping

Do you remember how we woke
to the first bird in that awkward pine

102

behind the ablution block, and leaned
across the knotted ground to lift
the canvas as though it was
the wall of the world
and ourselves at the heart of it
lying together
with the fresh grass against our faces
and the early air sweet beyond all telling –

do you sometimes look still
into that startled darkness
and hear the bird,
as I do?

When we drove away I looked back always
to the flattened yellow grass
to see the exact map of our imagining
our built universe
for a week
and saw that it was just earth
and faced the natural sky.

We took with us the dark pine
and the blackbird
and the dew beside our foreheads
as we woke

and now we live apart
and I don't know where they are.

On the Te Awamutu Road

It was a dark bird, silvery
in flight, coming quick
and awkwardly – low too, as though
already maimed; but that is useless
now to think of since without

apparent impact, no thud nor
syncopated interruption
of the wheels, I killed it.

I saw a turning tuft like black
and silver petals in the wind
and thought for something like a mile
that I should stop – and then
forgot. So it lies
without reproach, without defence
among the larger carelessnesses
left about my life.

Before First Light

Sometimes I imagined the morning I would wake
early, see the sycamore outside our window
moving against the visible blue dark
and turn to find the familiar misery
set hard, carved as the features of your face.

And it would seem that death was
an affirmation, a final payment
dissolving our drifting debt, proof
after all of the firmness of our contract;

you would lie like stone, raising
no further objections; not raging, not weeping
we would be seen at last to agree.
Even the unpassionate gods who observed
our torment would sigh for us then.

You woke and turned, frowning,
the dawn wind shook the leaves;
did I suppose that death is to be rehearsed
any more than staying alive?

Revelations

For so long you thought you understood money
– that rage against materialism,
a healthy cynicism towards the corruptible rich
even your deprecating smile
when you explained the fur coat
was really your mother's . . .

Money, it's a vulgar relation,
improvident, shifty, mixed up with ratbags,
who knows, perhaps even junkies –
how he's always admired you though,
given you substance, as he whined and drifted
while you went neatly to the office
and in the evenings got asked out
to dine at decent restaurants –

now you're out of work you've lost your shine,
you watch how much he eats,
scowl when he asks for the odd cigarette;
you're not so amusing either (was that given too?)
and though the silk blouses have lasted
you don't wear them with much style
these days. And your dreams!
How ignoble they are, how boring – all streets,
and as for that one that repeats itself
with the laughing behind you . . .

Ah, it's beautiful, money; it has a capacity
for selfless admiration, wants to build you up,
it's used to being disgusting itself
and immoral – everything's done for you.
Actually, it's the best friend you had.
Why didn't you recognise it
all the time it was there?

Threads

I sat up late those years
stitching small girls' dresses
– skirts as full as flowers
to be drawn on single cotton
inch by fragile inch
till tight enough for bodices
cut close about
those unvoluptuous chests.

At twelve or one
under an overcoat of sleep
I bent to my slight momentous craft
not daring urgency
or the ample bunching broke
and fell fumbled on my knee;
the clock snapped for malice
on the shelf. It's quiet tonight

again I sense thread's fine and tensile pull
– it's held for eighteen lines
and now (dresses had always to be hemmed
and pressed for school) I must draw
the ends together. Words too
can serve for comeliness and fit
when you or I set out
across the morning of the world.

Girls

This top is the pitch of the world
and they've got there, two girls golden
as stamens of wheat, their bicycles burning
– all still now and tingling
receiving their fierce anointing of sun.

Past the high towns they came
Te Pohue Tarawera
tossed on the horn of the hill
past the rivers Rahunga Rangitikei Mohaka
past the sheep seen creeping like maggots
up tracks to the osier's body of shade –

now they stand shining
proclaiming Look! I'm alive!
I've got red hair that tilts
at the tips, I've got freckles
a melon-slice grin
– or I'm taller, more sallow
with boy's hips and a frizz . . .

we've arrived, we're located
we've found an address at the centre
of four horizons
a hawk hung in one corner
and a cattle truck dripping with dung
rolling by . . .

They are bright dust, two sparks
in a travelling galaxy
spun to this moment
for taking a sip of eternity
pause on the road to the hillsides of thunder
Turangakuma Titiokura – yes, yes
they know they're at last for the dark.
But look how they blaze in the light.

The Comforting

You come limping a little
out of the cut-throat yard
into my curtained room

I am ready at once, drop everything
to talk; out there dust settles
savage faces turn away

I press home my advantage
with advice, carefully phrased –
you raise your head

smile with a curious coldness:
had I forgotten then
that hurt brutes may bite?

The Circumstance

I remember the rain
how it roared on the roof
while we ran from window to window
like children, exclaiming
watching it slide
lopsided from a bend
in the green gutter pipe
and dance on the ground.

Slowly the room darkened
and closed around us
each moment still holding
the wonder of rain.
In the morning a cicada sang
in the wet leaves –
for nothing, really;
for glory.

The National Poetry Series: Michael Ryan

I want to go to America, I want to listen
again to the drawly voices
in the glitter and sprawl of 7th Avenue

43rd, Broadway, the crumbly park
where one lunch hour I gobbled
a fat tuna fish sandwich
just down from Madison Ave

I slept in a tawdry hotel
with gold fleur-de-lis on scarlet paper
all over the foyer and a cross Greek
guarding the phone
and I wrote down all the names of airlines
in the subway coming in from J.F.K.
Aviaco Alitalia Lufthansa Balair
Pilgrim Air France Guyana Finnair . . .

But here is this poet of thirty years
saying 'No one can tell you
how to be alone' – his youngster
is swinging on the fence, it's his birthday
there's a nice guy across the street
he isn't alone, at all

not as I am (women should stay by their men
grow stout with listening)
this young bearded fellow
has continents of living ahead of him
yet knows the bleak journey

I don't know the way, I shall trip
and fall down in America
and it's the one place
where they're crass enough to leave me
wherever I land
disgrace, they will know,
being what we were born to.

Roly's Poem

It worked hard
making intricate angular gestures
with rhymes and references
as it stalked towards the page.

'Too much intelligence' you thought
'too little simplicity'
wanting life to be easy
make friends with itself.

Tonight I know he is dead
suddenly
somewhere in Switzerland. I see
his square walk
his jaunty, oblique, unfinished grin

and I want much more than this for him
not silence
for his elaborations
nor such report
to make him plain

– but it was his poem, after all;
he must always have stood too far back
for our touching.
I wish I had said I liked him.

Composition with Window and Bulldozer

Come outside, here's the quick world
noisy, inconsequential, brash
its engine rapping against
the rowdy noon (up to the elbows
in rubble on our reeling hill)

but the sun! What luck
to be here, holding on
to this shabby beach-ball of a planet
spinning under the sun's
brilliant umbrella
so we glint like bright grains
as it passes

I turn to the window
and see us – small girl, black hair
polished by light (behind, the rude clacking
still knocking the hill)
and myself, tall woman taking her turn
in the brief incandescence:
look how they stretch in it
reach for it –

oh yes little girl
laughing and shining
we are in it together. Even you
do not have very long in the sun.

The Action

By the long window you ponder
standing quite still so I see
how your body's alert with
the wakeful spring
of twenty-three years – ready
to move the great questions
to some place that perhaps will
contain their facets of pain;

love, work, they are there, the name
you can give to your God, oh and money,
the children it's said you will have
(and to what will you give yourself
wholly, where hold back, when you soften
how will you yield) – they are
the boulders you have yet to heave,
shoulder, shove, to urge somehow ahead.

As for me, I keep talking. Over and over
(mine are quite close to me now)

I finger them, changing the names
asking questions that echo
with queer insistence about my head.

The sun comes obliquely,
bronzed and muscular ally it stands
beside you, my daughter.
Now you are going outside together.

Bicycles

I have a dream of bicycles
of the shine on us when we spin quickly
and how easily after a short wobble
we capsize, and sprawl ignominiously.
Some I know believe in decoration,
winding rufflettes of crêpe paper
into their spokes and waving gloriously
as their pierrot suits billow by;

I see too how we keep changing speed
(but only by remembering the principles
of balance) and there is a head wind
to consider, or the one behind driving hard
on our backs – is it luck, that,
or care in choosing the route?

Today you've drawn up beside me
and put your foot to the ground –
I've stopped too, we have everything
to say; it's thrilling, even though
we are constantly interrupted
by the noise of the larger traffic. Still,
this is a love poem – though
at another time it could be a lament
and if we stayed long enough
on this corner for the whole world
to loiter beside us and pass the time of day
that would compose an epic.

As it is, it's just a moment
before we leave the door
of the old second-hand shop, run
to get going, then take off into the wind
pedalling like mad; and alone.

The Susceptibility

So light, so quick
the solitary life
it's a rice silk scarf

a breath can turn it
lift, fill, let it fall.
It hung dead tonight

and then she came – she is
well! – he called (I
had waited) spring cried
in the buds of the silver birch
darkness crossed the grass

oh love   oh danger
the world spins fully round
in half an hour.

Fontana Rosa

A country railway station, much like
any other – Tutira, Otaki, Taneatua –
but the French grew larkspurs here

and yellow trumpets; beside it, awkward
extravagant, looms the Fontana Rosa.
It's a failed Norman castle

the tower adorned with pink flowers
looped tendrils, oranges lemons – a weird
mixture, the Fontana Rosa. Perhaps it's a joke.

But no, the Spaniard Ibañez wrote his tales
here, dreamed its excesses, dedicated it
to romanciers and the beauties of literature

Balzac, Dickens, Cervantes – their faces
are over the gate in ceramics.
Didn't he trust his own voice then

that he worried about turrets, enamel petals?
(he was certainly no designer) – they are
arguing now, it's become a local problem

the Spanish Government won't answer letters . . .
Don't listen amigo, from whatever baroque heaven
you are tinkering with now;

let it go in its time, the Fontana Rosa –
plantains are unpicking your pillars and only
spiders inhabit the halls of fame, but
I think, Ibañez, that the word endures.

On the Need to Hold a Driver's Licence

I came south after sunset
driving fast past the telegraph poles

near Mount Bruce the dark
walked out of the pine trees

and laid its hand on the farms
saying 'forget; forget'

but in the proud sky
the light stayed

114

I saw the long day there
its face bright with weeping

then the night took it in
and I drove on home.

Agricole

I can see him on the crown of the hill
Adam with sunburn and wrinkles
bending over his small windy lease
of the material universe
– fifth of an acre perhaps
of the Kaitoke foothills
that elbow the ranges for room

I've seen him before –
last year in a narrow blue valley
up country from Greymouth
one summer in the Rawene swamp
figure in bronze
in the simmering dunes of Te Kaha

I saw him in France too
in the lean plots behind the high villas
in the Alpes Maritimes
staking his peas on the slopes
below gilded Saint Agnes in April:

this is his place his adumbra
his palace, his poem
the holding beyond all possession
more brutal, more blunt than desire
– it's the weathered and salty old crone
moko on the chin
who comforts, instructs him
reproaches and punishes
she who at last without fuss
without quarrel
will quiet his complaining
and settle his heartbeat to sleep.

The Gift

We sat in a forward pew – she came
for me (though we had quarrelled earlier)
and there were superlatives
good clothes, prepared expressions;
I could not find my friend in anything
and did not want to weep

but all the time my companion
kept her stillness, as she does,
watching in her own way
and gradually I felt
an ease about my heart
that could flower into a natural sorrowing.

The dead must be allowed
to leave us wisely
with simplicity;
this young woman looked on
with a courteous unforced attentiveness.
She is my eldest daughter.

Driving from the Airport

Everywhere I see human colour
the pale skin of Evans Bay yachts
crowding frailly together
in wind beating over the water

a white spilling of daisies
down and down
upon the receiving hillside
and the burnt umber shadow
like floating hair underneath boat sheds

even the white arms of arrows
open on the road as I enter
the intersection. All this and I
– I am nothing
myself only, stopped by the road
with this pen this paper the cry of the wind
in the gorse

oh tell him
tell all those whose plane has gone
over the cold horizon
it is never a poem we want
never this plausible mask of smoke

it is the burning substance
the shiver
the sprawl
the full spectrum of light
on the poor bodily creatures
that are for ever misunderstanding the way
to be royally, ripely together.

The Chair

It's a high room at the top of stairs
the door closed
I know of nothing but the chair in the corner
hard wood, rounded, a kitchen chair
and the girl sitting, head bowed
not looking up to see
who has come or gone
but weeping, weeping.

She has wept like this all my life;
you don't have to go near her
nor wonder, inquire
she does not expect that
there have never been intimations of solace.

Down the usual road I keep walking
I am young, old, strong or sick; sometimes
I waver – it does not matter. The chair stays
and the girl
as though this is the whole world sitting
bending over the great aching club foot
of its sorrow, far back
in the closed room of my days.

The Henri Rousseau Style

Waking at this broad window I discover
every morning's green; the massed pohutukawas

sketch a sky as bright as malachite
the rain has lit a spider's web

with emerald reflections. It's
a Rousseau forest, the glass preserving

all that weird precision; only the beast
is lacking, murderous behind the leaves.

I turn away. Morning's for voices
lazy, low-toned, messing about

with tea and sugar spoons, recalling trifles
for 'perhaps' and 'mm-' for 'did I say . . . ?'

equivocations soft and slack
as tumbled bedclothes. To live alone

is to choose a static pageantry –
this silence that stares from corners

with its feral eyes and shows through
tawny fur the tips of predatory claws.

The Generations

The two trains grind and steady; stop.
Through rolling steam
your face clears
staring into mine.

We're not a yard apart,
I see your smooth cheek, eyes
round and confident
not much surprised.

I must do something! Yet you'll
not hear me shout through all
this glass – shall I gesticulate
point back there, so you'll

pay attention – look, I've been
into the mountains
I know how terrible the winters are
how treacherous the ice

I've felt the wind pitiless across
the rocks. I'm on my way back,
I'm in a position to . . . Ah that's
the bell! Slowly you're drawn away

looking ahead and smiling hopefully.
I'm moving too, in my direction –

you waved though – is it possible
you thought it kind of me to bother?

The Telephone May Ring at Any Moment

It's hard for you to tell me
that your cat is dead, proper to add
'of course you know I was neurotic . . .'

your voice enters a solitude already
shaped by the morning mail – a paper
beginning 'French sovereignty – '

some student's Christmas card
an exhibition opening – necessary cries
between the creatures that we are,

no more protected than a candle flame
before a windy door; it opens, and look –
a stupid taxi kills the friend you loved

and I, alone with messages, in turn
can offer nothing but a message;
so slight, so intermittent

is the life we know, to speak of 'order'
is mere optimism and 'natural law' simply
the daily terror in disguise.

Roseneath 1983

Walking in my suburb I am appalled
– eighteen stately houses
and every window empty, doors shut
against the mild December light
the Crescent blank as if it had been
dropped by inter-galactic accident –

what am I doing here this summer evening?
Learning again I suppose that
our lives are a worminess
of secret comings and goings
unblessed by the grace
a neighbourhood unthinkingly confers.

My friends I have not seen in these
nine years among you, where are
your faces, your creeping convoluted
animal selves – in drawers and cupboards?
stacked in lumber rooms
behind the panelled doors?

Ah we have lost our inheritance,
the tribal faith is gone – we live
and we shall die
alone behind the curtains that
divide us from the homeless thousands
the vivid cruel compassion of the street.

At Greenmeadows

Old roads have a life they cannot lose
though every house that some time
toed their line is carried off
by progress or decay. Once I meandered
home from school along this verge;
the haze on the summer sky is precise still
with childhood's halcyon poise,
its landmark the Sugar Loaf flares
with the remembered bright dead grass
each February ignites.

The alteration's mine. This road down which
my friend Joyce Paton dawdled towards
her gate, for years called 'Waipruss'
by us both, wears still its stick of wood
on the corner lamp post; 'Ypres'
the eye of my education reads
hearing now its slim French cadence –
and suddenly the whole of childhood's
confident innocence laughs with me
at its own delicious joke.

Enter a Messenger

It's true the fire would have been quick
– already it was catapulting across the hill
while I waved a hose at a wall
and saw over my shoulder (a queer languor
spreading inside the terror) how
it flung itself over the gorse
and came sprinting up on the wind.

They caught and drowned the thing
you know, within an hour; but this morning
regarding the dead trees
three or four yards from the house
I know it is only a matter of time
till it comes all the way:

some greater death it will be,
and after that I shall not come back,
but go where my weakness takes me
with the old undemanding quiet creatures
who are always there at the end – not you,
snapping with challenge and wit, nor
you running up the steps two at a time
while the silver dollar gum tree
brazenly whispers 'immortal . . . '

Anything would do to remind me,
but the fire did it; and I listened.
I take note. I remember.

September

The mountain leaps, and stands
breaking horizons. It is the first
land out of falling waters, the wind

finds it like a discovering dove.
In the wheeling light it is still,
construing containment, poise
from the inchoate idiom of the earth.

No flower was white before this
blossoming of snow, no September
sharp with spring until this morning.
I shall learn the lessons of God
from the mountain; it has entered
my imagination: eternal indifference,
eternal scope, eternal reprieve.

High Court Report

Morning sunlight shows
through my kitchen window
a mucky mild domestication
– old cartons bottles clay bank
with crooked steps a rusted hoe
awry on the crib wall's weeds.

In here, across the table
the skewed morning paper's
patched with words – 'knife'
I read, and 'blood'; 'woman',
'wardrobe where she cowered' –
then the paper folds

as though at the verb,
the act itself, it balked
afraid of its own utterance.
I look up. Outside
wild passionfruit is hung
with yellow tears

through smudged glass
the matipo's green constellations
after all are withered;

past harmless garbage bags
the path stumbles
bloodied at every step.

Tristesse d'animal

Here, yes, I am here –
don't you see my hand at the window, waving?

It's all still the same,
tremulous water lifting its face
to the wind, a clock calling over the city

light late on the hills –
and I'm alone, as before.

Where are you, companions
who promised to come
to the very door of the grave

– where did you turn back?
Are you dancing somewhere nearby

or is that only the neighbours?
I might call you
but what language is there for it

– the blood-smear we were born in
the gasp of that strong bitter oxygen
the first taste, the last we shall have.

I Cannot Chronicle our Love

nor yet keep silent. I am so entangled
in its conjuring nets –

they are the glittering strings
a top-hatted magician makes, eating
bright scarves and knitting them
behind his painted lips.

We talk of tenderness, but only
when you sleep do formal shadows
of the night reveal the grave unsmiling
sweetness of your face;

only then do I escape the call boys, footlights,
glare, the anticipations of the crowd
– our friends who wish to see
a spirited performance.

Oh love, we have forgotten
our simplicity. Those quiet, astonished
people that we were – where are they?
What have they become?

Prayer for Palliser Road

This valuable privacy
guarded by great facades
Chubbs burglar alarms over front doors
– I hope it is always beautiful
alight with, say, Woollaston landscapes
McCahon's salutary nightmares
making the owner humble

the air filled with Mahler, Shostokovitch
Debussy arabesques
on late summer afternoons
Lilburn's strict harmonies
to correct any carelessness of mind;

I hope too it quivers with the precision
of words honoured by Shakespeare Sam Johnson

Mark Twain and Mason, R.A.K. (to alleviate
sickness of soul from living
at a salubrious address). . .

but I am afraid that this treasured seclusion
estimated daily at up-market prices
may instead be limp with boredom,
the boorishness of the snubbed
or those doing the snubbing,
damaged by rage by inertia
pale with silliness
and indeed not so much a jewel at all
as a necessary presence
often idiot ungainly and small,
as mine is.

The Independent Outlook

A geranium lives the whole way
from root to flower, each cell
claiming a local autonomy.

Broken, plunged truncated
in stranger soil, it doesn't wait
for advice but blooms on the spot

though later I admit it's reduced,
a weedier thing while it learns new laws
practises foreign weather

but in a crisis I just love the way
each minute element of starfish leaf
pink capillaried skin-petal

manages its own department
and only on major questions (boundaries
say, the sharing of nitrogen, air)

will agree to wait till the word
of authority's ready at last to begin
weaving up from headquarters.

Pancakes for Breakfast

It is simply the mist
standing light and quiet
on the morning water

and I too am suddenly clear
having for weeks been embedded
in days as though
they had all set hard and I stuck
like an old turd in the clay path
where the children trample

but the mist is perfect
it has the shape and sheen of the harbour
in new sunlight
yet rests unafraid beside
the bright colonising sea

and I see how each other thing
gathers into its separate self
– the thin grass tufted on bog-coloured clay
a raw egg someone has dropped
rolling its small yellow wave
(absorbed as the hen herself, squatting)

yes, the egg is complete
– whether broken or whole –
as I am
walking with a slow joy over the hill
to buy cream from the early-opening store
to be whipped in the kitchen
and eaten with Barry's pancakes.

Playing House

I come in to the hot house
smelling of absence and dust
dead bumblebees on the sill
dry stalks, strange torpors
laying their heads on the air
sunlight ticking stilly
on yellow triangles of floor –

then the door from downstairs flies open
and she is here, my small friend
serious collaborator
in the comical business of living
– I mean, we know precisely
when money and things
are nothing but air in the hand
shop counters and shelves a mirage

but we know too that some things are real –
the present she's kept for me
tiny soap heart in a tin
a halcyon heart
perfect in her palm, in mine –
we gaze down, consider in silence
this grain of the dust of the stars
'You mustn't put that in the shop' she says
counting transparent money.

Well of course not. This is
an exact and judicious magic
– and I have come home.

From *Seasons and Creatures*

From the south

An orange flare of montbretia
briefly blazes by a fence
leaping past the car here,
and some duller embers beyond –
bracken I think – static, unconsuming
fevers that lightly enter the blood
as it courses in larger directions.

I am not even quite sure if that's
what they were, Monkey's Britches,
shoddy plebeians with bright lips
incurably parted, multiplying as they do
with indecent aplomb
on skinny verges, bulbs broad-bottomed
and hairy all over
cramming the dust down below –

and anyway they have vanished. Yet
they remind me, those public
fandangos, that our longings are themselves
a kind of happiness, a quick tilt
of attention at a spark obliquely caught
like a flash in the sun at a moving window,
glimpse of some passionate uncertainty
which is what we call daily living in these
nervous, unfinished, beautiful islands.

The outside room

It was the moon poised with a bright patience
low over the paddocks, the silence standing
about in surprise as though newly arrived,
the constant soft bleat of the sheep
and the earth, most of all the earth itself

sending up its unaccountably tender emanations
and winy smell, telling me what dew can do
to sap-heavy grass and sheep shit, and
to the sheep too, obscurely coiled
in the oily emollients of their wool –

all this, as I crept out in the no-time
after midnight, going to pee by the fence
squatting in the cool heady freshness, night's
elbow flung over the hill and the strange
spare light of the stars beyond –

all whispering, explaining, declaring
that the persecuted earth has not yet
resigned its ancient romance with seasons
and creatures; and so clearly my body
couldn't help exulting as it tiptoed back

over the cold crush of the grass, stones
by the door, and I saw without looking the dark window
behind which the young lay asleep together
holding once again safe until morning
their dream of a lifetime to come.

Rain in the hills

The dead stay with you always
taking house-room, finding in you
their haven and harbour; and this happens
even though you know their going sealed off
for you a segment of the whole circle
of things and now wherever you walk there is
some part of the hills and sky
you do not see, though it is not
obscured by the seasons or weather:

but where you are, in this impaired place,
they also remain and are necessary
and beautiful as the thundery light
over the black spurs on an evening
of spring rain; and being there
they will change, not as images
of yourself but in their own way,
allowing you to perceive them
with a fresh vision again and again.

Even the terrible deaths you believed
would shrink your heart forever
do not come to an end or leave you,
for you cannot repudiate your suffering
– it is in you, it is what you have become:
the limited world of loss is still
your support, your delight, and as real
as this hill angled with black stone
and the violet clouds above it –

they are yours, stately and strange
as they are, holding your defeat
and your knowledge of defeat, which is also
entirely at home in you, in how you
watch and speak, in your composition,
your nerve pathways, your membranes
and cells. This is the chemistry of pain.

The Noh plays

'Three months,' they said in July
but it is November and you are here still
gaunt on the pillow, your eyes
following us, pleading not so much for us
to settle your question but to know
how a man might give up his asking.

For us too the time is defined –
this is the last act: we cannot afford
a single careless gesture.
In your room at given positions
we are poised in a watchful patience.
The white window dare not close its eye.

In the Noh plays of Japan death is not
mentioned, but a character speaks
as a ghost bearing the soul of a man
– one who has endured his torment
in the Three Worlds of nature
and earned his release;

he plays out his suffering, his folly,
his search for wisdom; at last
his voice dims. Out of the silence
a young man begins to recount
new and remarkable exploits. But these are
the first words of another cycle.

Orthopaedic ward

With you in these clean rooms
are the secret creatures
'living in millions'
as Sister observes
'in your mouth, ears,
nostrils'; disporting themselves no doubt
in the lush spongy jungles
of everyone's hair:

a below-stairs society
settled in blind unicellular hierarchies
manifesting its potency
with the greatest indifference
– no question but living's
for staying alive, and killing
as necessary and plain
as hospital pyjamas – a truth

we are learning here
among trolleys of folded linen
stacked crutches, wounds
swelling with newly invented species,
the spectre of amputation
stalking the corridor after lights out.
'Good luck for yours,' says our jovial anguish
as each trolley trundles off

to another trial by oblivion
and we put an ear to the wall
as though we could pick up the murmur
of hordes that can simply increase
till they help themselves
to everything that we are –
barbarians silently massing
at the gate of the matchless city.

The lecture

I am just going downstairs to where
I shall tell them lies. Up here
at the window the maple trees' shadow

fingers the indigo dusk and the fireflies
carry their tiny cargoes of light
up, down, right to the ground, then

almost over the high branches again
riding their currents of bark-scented dark
with an unquestioning poise

giving off sparks from a wholesome
summer travail. I could watch them
all night; what I cannot do

is burn at the small purifying fires
of their industry. I shall go soon,
persons are waiting to hear what I claim

that I know. I will talk down, say
'in respect of', offer insights, despising
both them and myself, but thinking:

'Up there in the quiet room
where the fireflies are to be seen
at work in their luminous trees

there is my truth, my candour, my courage,
there I too can shine with the natural
intermittent light of myself,'

– and then I shall go on holding forth.

Cows

I followed the by-pass road behind Woodville
the sky as clean as a cut apple
around me the milky and putrid smell of cows
– in the rise of the dew, cows steaming
and wandering, slung from their frames
like black and white blankets
hung out to dry. They do say
you can make milk from grass, without cows
and their warm galumphing machinery
and tunnelly stomachs . . . Bah! at the thought
steam bursts in an angry spiral
straight up from a cake of shit
and the small ears twitch and shudder
above the luminous heads.

Or so I say. But these are the real,
the solid cows that cannot quarrel
or kill, have never fallen in love
and could not defend the dumb expertise
of their milk-making, which they did not invent
and do not observe with the least interest,
any more than they remember in autumn
how they roared all night in the spring
when their calves were taken away.

They do not suppose this matters,
nor that anything else does – indeed,
they do not suppose. Their time is entirely
taken up with the delicious excruciating
digestion of existence
and if they please me on the by-pass road
in the ripening sun this morning
that is wholly my affair.

The ghost moth

Once we lived so close to the bush
each day wore the beech trees' rangy profile,
all night the creek purred, brushing
the antennae of our sleep; in the evening
moths came pouring into the lamplight,
some small, blue-sheened, as though it was
light itself combed to dust on their wings

or a ghost moth stared from the doorway
sheathed in its gentle shallow gaze;
and we ourselves seemed diffused like
the light, and would wander away
past the moths to the leaf-shivering trees
as though summoned in secret
by the morepork's comfortless cry.

That earthy unearthly life is over now
but sometimes still when you come in
from the purposeful street and hesitate,
blinking, I think of the moths
how they wheeled into the lamp's bright
aureole and turned and turned, dazzled
by something they never really saw.

An orange cat

Come into the little wooden towns
walk with me, covertly watched
by for instance Mrs McGrath in the dairy
and Walter O'Connor dreaming his luck
on the TAB's peeling old seat,
wander the road a mile wide
to Major and Major Solicitors
unseen behind the dim frosted square
of their window, last painted in 1949

see where the poplars are greening
alongside the camping ground
and the white wooden church standing
drier than Danny O'Dowd
before the bar opens up at eleven –

dry too the ancient verandahs
shrunk by a century's seasons
on cottages built when the plain was a forest
the towns no more than depots
for horses and men at large on a wooded island
twelve thousand miles from home;

it was all trees, it was timber
and timber it still is,
and the sweet slummocky smell of the sun
on doorways and porches, Sally McCutcheon
in grey perm and a cardigan
getting along in her slippers,
Mick Griffin rolling his own at the entrance
to *Saddlery All Leather Goods Ltd*
and an orange cat lazily limbering up
on the other side of the road.

The sums

Somewhere you are always going home;
some shred of the rag of events
is forever being torn off and kept
in an inside pocket or creased satchel
like the crayon drawing, blurred now,
you frowned over once in a desk:

it's kept for the moment when you go
mooching along the verandah and through
the back door, brass-handled, always ajar,
to where the floured apron stands monumental
above veined legs in a cloud of savoury steam,
mince, onions, the smell of childhood's Julys;

there again you are quick-flounced and shrill
shrieking on a high stool the answers
to sums – multiplication, addition, subtraction,
all the mysteries known as 'Mental' – alchemy
that could transmute 48 + 17 (when you got it,
yelling) to a burst of fire in the blood –

it is still there, still finding its
incorruptible useless answers,
your life's ruined verandah, the apron,
the disfigured legs that with a stolid
magnificence used to hold up the world.

Tempo

In the first month I think
it's a drop in a spider web's
necklace of dew

at the second a hazel-nut; after,
a slim Black-eyed Susan demurely folded
asleep on a cloudy day

then a bush-baby silent as sap
in a jacaranda tree, but blinking
with mischief

at five months it's an almost-caught
flounder flapping back
to the glorious water

six, it's a song
with a chorus of basses: seven, five grapefruit
in a mesh bag that bounces on the hip
on a hot morning down at the shops

a water-melon next – green oval
of pink flesh and black seeds, ripe
waiting to be split by the knife

nine months it goes faster, it's a bicycle
pedalling for life over paddocks
of sun
no, a money-box filled with silver half-crowns
a sunflower following the clock
with its wide-open grin
a storm in the mountains, spinning rocks
down to the beech trees
three hundred feet below
– old outrageous Queen Bess's best dress
starched ruff and opulent tent of a skirt

packed with ruffles and lace
no no, I've remembered, it's a map
of intricate distinctions

purples for high ground burnt umber
for foothills green for the plains
and the staggering blue
of the ocean beyond
waiting and waiting and
aching
with waiting

no more alternatives! Suddenly now
you can see my small bag of eternity
pattern of power
my ace my adventure
my sweet-smelling atom
my planet, my grain of miraculous dust
my green leaf, my feather
my lily my lark
look at her, angels –
this is my daughter.

The capable spirit

Oh yes happiness arrives all right,
it set itself up here last Friday
adopting like Maui all necessary forms
to suit the present adventure

chattering in the weatherboards
of a lean-to kitchen, rustling like paper
in tacked bright prints on the walls
gloating over our shoulders
at these complete little feet
faint-stroked eyebrows
half-cat's-eye pale shell fingernails
unfocused blue eyes;

try animal, mineral, vegetable, this is
the most various magic any of us will know;
in a bedscape of milky breast
it moons and whispers, goes to perch
on a yellow bucket in the bathroom

rash phantom pretending to command
all the great ceremonies in this one;
and it does seem just now, in this flimsy cottage,
it can do anything. Clever with love,
it is busy composing a life.

Hymns Ancient and Modern

On a rough night spinning past
the macrocarpas' violent shadows
wind wrenched the car sideways
till for very apprehension I began singing
the purposeful hymns of childhood
All Hail the Power   O Worship the King
Su-un of my So-oul Thou Sa-aviour Dear

mist sent its wraiths whirling
queerly over the farms as I intoned
Rock of Ages, even at last Lest We Forget
(oh the smell of chrysanthemums
on terrible Anzac Days!).

But truly on Tinakori Hill
the dark spurs motioned me past
and I came on home. Up steps to the windy door
key in the lock   the first light switch
mail in a pile on the table
your letter.

'It happened last week, in England.
The children have been told.'
Six-year-old Josie, died of a brain tumour.
A small child, pretty, inclined to giggle
– that's really all I know.
How silent the wind is
it has no voice now
no song. It is just wind, after all
just air
the cruel and stupid air that will always
come and go at random –

in All Saints Sunday School
at a death we sang Abide With Me
in our effortless thin voices

and looked out the window
savouring all the Sunday dinners
still to come.

The process

In a time of desolation
to recall the rich acres of summer
is to know you are alone; the others
have gone, or changed irrecoverably –

it is as though change itself
is the auctioneer who put under the hammer
a precious expanse, knocking it down
to the bead-bright eyes of loss, illness
separation, death –

so we no longer lean on our elbows
at Frank's narrow table, his trout mornay
steaming under the lifted spoon
nor sprawl in the study
where poems burgeoned and broke
against Mexican embroideries,
Meg stumbling over our legs as she
ran out, weeping, and Vincent spoke
of white horses in a manic moonlight
somewhere in the Cotswolds – while all the time

outside lay love's precarious landscape
ours without act of possession
the place that, as we talked,
time had already noted yard by silent yard
and marked for sale by dissolution.

A reckoning

You were my friend, accomplice in
the copious plotting parents are a party to;
through centuries of jovial boredom
on the beach we stuck it out together

then separately awake hallucinated
over teenage accidents in cars, until
a door at last breathed out and cracks
of guilty silence shot us dead asleep.

Our fears kept us close; pride too,
and the small events' unmerciful momentum.
It was a walled garden, safe to quarrel in,
love coming down on us reliably as rain.

We were its keepers, so intent we did not see
the change of sky, the gradual departures
– then there was just a man, a woman
slamming some old gate on a quiet plot

ill-tempered without learnt weather
and the rule of law. Who were
the guardians then, and who, despite
that virtuous authority, the guarded?

At the hospital

I thought him much older, a gentleman
of style, neat black moustache, debonair
hand waving across the corridor

from his cotton-quilt corner to mine;
the fluffy girl who stayed so long by his bed
reading as though at home must be his daughter.

'Got it all sussed out,' he'd call
over the breakfast trays, his legs
a white mountain hiding the strict machinations

of surgeons, 'told the boss I'll do
his job lying down, lucky bastard he is . . .'
and at once he was young, just a boy.

'Twenty-one,' murmured the girl, bringing
us all ripe peaches, 'his brother's a haemophiliac
too,' and we understood how each act

could touch off the treacherous bleeding. Days
they prepared him for theatre drawn curtains
kept everyone quiet; I considered

my own wound, superficial, properly healing;
he began to look further away
and the waving grew smaller. On the last day

I gave him my macadamia nuts. 'You'll be fine,'
and he grinned, jaunty like his own boss,
like an uncle, like anyone living for ever –

I walked quickly, but it was a hard mile
to the big double doors at the corner
and Sister, nodding and smiling goodbye.

Epithalamion

for L.E.R.

Wife, woman, hausfrau, female companion
you are rightly summoned again
to the careful ceremony. But you know,
you never left off being married
as you went on guarding your supplies
(ripening figs, soup stock, pears
to be bottled) with a gentle managing tact
somehow avoiding the crowd of waiting
ambitions while you nourished the cells
of the house – a grandchild's teddy bear
the failing lassiandra bushes . . .

wife, wif, woman, let me re-define the notion
stand it before me, observe
the natural wave of its greying hair
the unclamorous refrain of the voice
and the confident smell of a cleaned kitchen
the labelled jars glinting, a whiff
of cut grass at the window –

yes the wife in you, widowed, kept up
its daily preparation of house room
for the heart, stayed mysteriously content
with the ancient humilities
a lit fire, a boiling kettle
the deep solace of bread.

Still

On December evenings you walk into the house
quite simply, smiling inwardly as you did,
a nearly nonchalant ghost

choosing – for you have more choice
than I'd have supposed – those
fading gold six o'clocks

we wandered through to sit
on the balcony, narrow and gritty
as it was; and took in

the complicated scents of the gum tree
and were washed by the light
of a mellow impermanent sky.

Coming through

Beautiful woman laughing
throat quivering in this smudgy light
back arching, the tide of delight
rising in you like a transfusion;
your breasts ripple like blown grass
– the good one, and the other
made of scars and contraptions –

you never laughed like this before,
taken over, lost in it (there are tears
on your face): you're adrift now
each day's a fresh notice
that your moorings have been untied
and you're out on the swell

you can take any direction:
now your maimed body has given up planning
it's abandoned
to its narrow, blue-green, lace-flounced
elegant incomplete present –

next time I must make an appointment
I have to take my chances;
in your understood freedom
you are already
half out of sight.

Camellias

1: Femme de lettres

Today was small and precious
each ellipse of sunlight
sidling across your hair
and eyebrows, the beard you tug
between other grander gestures;

the glossed camellia leaves
stood still, poised as though to be
the more exquisitely excluded
along with the pale petals we did not
notice as intently we leaned and talked

each word brighter-bodied for
the shadow of the ones we did not say
– this is after all the edited life
to cut, to prune, select, is my profession
– I did not know such practice

could command a lazy room of polished leaves
and sun. Even your kiss ached
with a sweet forfeited knowledge;
behind us waited those still, crisp stalks,
the flowers a single breath can tarnish.

Camellias

2: Working

A rough morning, wind thumping the house
and all about it these bustling bodies
shoulders sawing up sunlight in chunks
hands scrabbling and beating the clay
of my lumpy hillside; three young men
I have asked to conceive it as garden
their flung shouts whirling
along corridors of the wind.

Older, I stay inside (besides, I am
paying) here where camellias are stuck
in a pot and Wilhelmina, young too
and inextinguishably cheerful, is cleaning
my windows. What a season is spring –
raw, hyperactive, blatantly kind
reeking like sweat of the future:
did I too once take the season full on

like a fist, like a kiss, like
a drowning . . . ? Look, the flowers
have fallen, they lie like pink
crumpled skin on the floor, but the leaves,
the unyielding bright leaves, are
making a stand. I likewise turn back
to my desk, to this page, to you,
to hear how my poem tells you.

After dark

There was some pain, but afterwards
I slept; and then my body found itself,
grew warm, flirtatious even, left
to open the door to an austere stranger:
'Charming, my dear,' he stepped inside,

'your skirt's alluring swing, gestures
of comprehension, style . . . but, you know,
these things do not matter now; I want
instead what all of this conceals –

I desire your very flesh, so keenly
I shall peel it from the bone, your eyes
I'll close, your mouth silence with my kiss:
you will in turn receive the one entire,
absolute possession.' Then he left.

My body found his card and took it up
but quickly put it down; the object was
unpleasant, strangely textured,
harsh and wordless; black.

He had already said he'd call again.

Dunedin in July

After fifty the mind's muscles begin to
slacken, the view it encompasses grows
broader, yet I think more lightly held.

This morning on a cold Otago hillside
I take in Mount Cargill, snow beard
untrimmed, the spires of sober churches,

the steely light of the sky, near me
in black earth under the ngaio tree
a single snowdrop two inches high;

and in the same moment, precisely set
in its narrower frame, the same hill sprinkled
with beech tree shadow in summer

a young woman walking and watching
beginning thirty years ago to learn
all I have inescapably become.

She is quiet and merry and spry, secure
in the power she has no idea
she will lose or relinquish repeatedly

in the anguish of later seasons –
she is so close I can almost touch her
nearly smile into those unseeing green eyes;

behind her the hills and the city
tilt and steady in the piercing southern light
as though to confer the outline

of one horizon on older and more confused,
more hurtful angles. Standing here
I can just smell the scent of that flower.

The invasion

So this is what it is like –
nothing here, where I live,
but news from a distance
coming like a report from the front
of the ravages of action
to those appalled at base.

I have no power to re-deploy
that innocent violence
– it is hard enough to believe in it –
skin like an old pullover
dragged over the head, crumpled
in scornful caricature
of a lifetime of moods
breasts meek as a boy's, mocking
their vanished opulence, bones taut
in a thinning garment of flesh

– it's a disguise cast in derision
a badly managed facsimile
spurious in its authority. I am
a country divided, taken over
by the invader, bounded by
insulting frontiers.

Yet I have my Resistance
my government in exile
a cabal of one to fight my
undercover battles; no one can
stop me giving the orders. In here
I shall fight my life to the death.

From *Summer near the Arctic Circle*

The Written Word

Leaving's a little death. Packing,
I see already its wake of signs
and messages, to be witnessed
by another woman who will draw
my long red curtains, take books from
my shelves, sleep in my bed.

Cards left on the window sill
are leaning, a bit drunk, very knowing,
ripe with love and friendship's
intimate knowledges of me
which they won't bother to conceal
or care if they distort, for her.

So it must surely be
with a whole existence's accumulations;
the pronoun that begins our breath,
the violent 'I', becomes at last
a dissolving froth of words
that follows us away

and others will of right come in
and occupy our days and nights
and breathe our air and walk about
the great rooms of the world
when they have cleared away
the litter of our correspondences.

Counterpoint

Swift, fatal, this thundery light
on the hills
like a proof of the end of the world
visible emanation
from the virulent arsenals
growing like maggots
under the earth's accountable skin;

yet how beautiful the soft-lit city
– look, the moon's taking off now
careering away past the pine trees
and here in the hedge
see the cool green of taupata leaves
each a small plate of moonlight
tilting towards the dark:

it's our earth and city, our place,
loved and illusory possession
brief habitation, oasis
in the violent nomadic passage
a careless species takes
across its given star.
This is its song.

Going to the Grampians

Kangaroo – best get it over with,
the absurd word. It works though
for the creature's lopsided profile
as it sits on its own triangle
of elbows and tail, the weak nose
facing forward, baby fingers hanging down,

all the bulk behind, below
nothing to speak of in the apex
of a head
a hairy geometrical outrage
to every upright Australian.

But if you go into the hills
follow eucalyptus-shadowed roads past
the sudden enormous rocks, and see them
at home in a clearing
cosseting their children
with delicate small hands, or as lovers,
he stroking, paws lingering tenderly
over her bowed head,
she sitting and trembling;

the animal in you is quiet too
before creatures you thought ridiculous,
acknowledging a kind of grace
in an alien desire that uses
our most intimate gestures, brutes blessed
by the bodies they know as
love's most true, most wholesome domain.

At Bywell

This earth is dense with days, lived through
and left behind in long-repeated seasons.
We read of villagers who 'in these parts'
received the travellers who walked
the Roman Bridge across the Tyne
a thousand years ago, bringing
Border gossip, news no doubt of
the murdering Scots not sixty miles away.

Hushed on this later summer afternoon
by their remote yet homely presences,
we walk the spongy grass with some idea,
I think, of treading lightly on a soil
so pungently composed; passing each other
heads down, pondering our closeness
above the churchyard ground to those
who've gone within with all their gear –

the woven tunics, mantles, breeches,
heel-less shoes, the treasured oxen, children's
breakfast bowls, the sunlit harvestings
of barley, groats; round smoky kitchens
jumpy with tallow flames, their bright
or clouded eyes . . . foolish to think we hear them
in the shadow of the limes – and yet
they do speak, for a moment, when we stand

by the north wall, close enough to touch
the dusty stone, mellow as trapped sunlight
– surely it's their prayers we hear, as in
the squat Saxon tower we see their knuckling down
to the severer ecstasies of God. In the nave
I touch with a kind of shyness the frosterly
marble column – black sheen with grey
stone flowers alive, alight within it.

Summer near the Arctic Circle

Midnight and still light, Leningrad and I
awake to another white night, that spare
other world where each leaf and stone
is not to be approached, scarcely named,
so rare, so unearthly has it become.

Somewhere there must be a temperate time,
the plain night and day that I know, and there
I imagine the green oval of some tiny park
glowing dewy and crisp, lovers walking
just such a path as this, reaching up

to real blossoms (tree-sized narcissi,
white, scentless), the gold dome of a solid
St Ives, as grand, that gleams
in a simple cycle of night-times and noons.
This is more strange: time, caught

in a soft frost of seasons, has left us
outside the door of the days, strangers
to ourselves, opaque shapes in some
neutral clarity – we can't call it light –
on the other side of the air. Half afraid,

I touch the bright grass, dandelion-studded,
the white flowers that perch on the trees,
and hear incommunicable whisperings
from a white Polar noonday stalk the silence
between the Russian lovers and me.

The Internationals

The tall Canadian is drunk
all the more gleefully for being
four thousand miles from home; each of us
tolerates his hot confidentiality
even rather enjoying the flop of long arms
randomly about us

but the black African's mask is very smooth
his murmurings musical, remorseless the kiss
that fixes, holds each breathless woman
in turn, till the backs of other men's heads
say squarely *Go away man can't you just*
fucken go away . . . something is running
among us, small and dangerous as the scorpions
that glitter in corners, black and quick
in this fierce Aegean climate

'He's no good!' hisses the blurry North American
and turns and seizes
the everlastingly smiling fellow
and pushes him down, down
– it's a joke
an embrace
a scuffle, the laughter is shrill and silly
and black man's subsiding
as though under a lover
wanting him
wanting the savage caress
of that contemptuous body –

'D. H. Lawrence . . .' somebody mutters
in a second of silence
and at last we begin to disentangle
the two creatures, in slow motion they slide
separately out of perspective.

Catching nobody's eye
we talk in a spent monotony
of the World Cup
– or is it the French Grand Prix.

Rhineland

I walked in the early morning
down the path by the water, and there
I could smell the old river smell

of the brimming Rhine, hear
its purposeful lapping, see the long barges
linked together GEFO TANK2GEFO ROTTERDAM

out already, plugging steadily on,
and brown-stained, long abused as it is,
the capable waterway taking on yet another

of its numberless days for shouldering
Europe's cargoes, bearing its poisons
on that wide and glistening back;

and it was as though it turned and looked up
from its liquid trudging, to remind me
that a continent's dying still richly harbours

the knowledge of ancient endurance – which
I acknowledged, nodding to the Old Survivor,
though all round me the elderberry flowers

narrowed, going down with their season
and the faintly acrid-scented may sprigs,
dying too in their own stiff arms.

Train Song

Deep in the night they call out from the mountains,
they are stirring the bowl of black winds in the mountains,
now they blow a long braying thunder beside me,
they elbow and stamp through my pasture of sleep;

the eternally purposeful even-keeled trains, how
they conceive absolutely their duty, their scope,
how they bow their great heads to be timetabled, tamed,
with what giant composure they all measure up.

It is evening, it is raining – on palm leaves,
on the iron gates, the orange tree branches, the tiny
green lilies that push through the stones, on the hand
I hold out. It is raining now all over Europe;

and slowly in sleekness with sheen on the rails
my trains sinew by me and eerily peer –
grave with surprise are the faces of trains
and helpless in turn my white face at the door.

The trains go to Venice, Brindisi, Geneva,
on to the Caucasus, Russia, Mongolia;
passing, they are passing, it is day it is dark
and my dear ones are sleeping; I will never go home.

Directions

When you slipped in beside me
I wanted to hold you completely,
make one entire, encompassing gesture;
but you remain always a foreign country,
a place where my papers permit me
explorations, also familiar journeys
that may again discover
love's recognizable landmarks

as one might come to a piazza
in a remote and beautiful city
remembering evenings when the violinist
swayed to his song and the black-brimmed
magician strode round his invisible circle
and touched his lips to the crowd
and then called softly in
the expectant dusk his *Ah, fantastica!*

Fremantle, February '87

In the wake of the fast craft, the Twelve Metres,
flaunting illustrious flags and the expensive gear
of the Cup Race, creep in the poets: no crowds
now, but the tidied up posh hotels take us in

with a polite resignation. 'Liked the *glitterati*'
grins the lift boy, offering his nostalgia
gratis, as he bundles us in – ordinary folk,
slightly anxious about luggage, inclined

to go through the wrong door, visibly dazed
by opulent expanses of carpet, palm fronds,
velveteen chairs. Clearly we are no great cop
– and who was it booked us in? Arts what?

Yet we have our moment of glee, alone
in the temporary palaces of our rooms
when we smile strangely at this unlikely
location, knowing we belong at ground level

among the rank, the wormy, the unsmart, we
the infiltrators, saboteurs, remorseless pursuers
of dirt under the carpet, investigators without
permission; that they allow us in at their peril.

Green

The young woman wearing a knickerbocker suit
of elegant dull green walked, slender, slow,
gripping a stick on which she almost leaned
but not to alter a scrupulous erectness.

I came abreast; her eyes looked straight ahead
as though to find each separate step
by an unwavering vigilance; I glimpsed
the long gaunt cheek tanned by make-up,

felt the quivering white electricity
of will that could so charge
a dying animal that had already shrunk
into a long-desired exhaustion

and so present it, masked and chic,
with the whole length of the world to walk
before the seething footlights of Fifth Avenue
on a summer afternoon at five o'clock.

Commonwealth Poetry Tour

One: an awkward blunt man from Zambia
stiff with allegiance to the honourable
African cause; two: the Indian gentleman,
small, exquisite, lit by cultivated obsessions,
and we three who sat with them hour by hour
in difficult English trains and joked, gossiped,
quoted, presenting our foreign selves
in this oddly thrown together confederacy;

each evening another destination, shy strangers
approaching the train, parties to follow,
ourselves reading poems in small halls, proceeding
to dim or determined receptions, to sleep, tea
in the early morning, another railway platform,
more tired, more excited, and in the end
so close it seemed we could have known
no other life, no companions before these five.

So it grew, tiny convincing universe
feeling its frailty, marvelling at its passion:
see us lean forward as green fields slide by
the train rocking to the rhythms of our
absorption, hear us name our momentous loyalties
– the code, to care for one another,
to honour the shared occasion – eight minutes each
on the stage has the force of a cosmic law.

Look now at one more blank assembly, and
the young Indian forgetting us and himself, reading
on and on like a madman in a dismayed silence,
and as he sits down the touchy African, white-lipped
'If you do that again I'm leaving this tour . . .'
Witness our serious grieving, the pacifying
and comforting, the troubled dispersing
to the usual anonymous houses; and once again

in the morning, the train, we three surrounding
the sorrowful transgressor, explaining now,
defending, putting the case, eagerly piecing
together a pattern of forgivable rage,
the spare Zambian silences being, we say,
much further away than our mild solitudes
from the present intensities, intimate
and compelling as hospital friendships –

and yes, he's restored by this careful compassion,
our love after all not tarnished, victory
worthily won and acknowledged – and then
– O miraculous consummation – see the door open
feel the cold blast, the shudder and rattle,
and he's here, striding forward hand outstretched,
his African Englishman's voice deep with appeal
'. . . dreadfully rude . . . forgive me . . . your hand . . .'

This story has no deaths and endings,
no nightmares even, it's scarcely a drama at all,
but look, take a last glimpse of us, foolish
no doubt in our childish elation, see the shine
in the eyes, tender curving of lips as, quiet now
and near tears, men and women of dust and division,
we are touched by the spirit, the life
breathed newly, holily, into our clay.

Driving through the Gorge

No one enjoys this road; it's narrow,
in winter the river below turns
a yellow cold shoulder on your attempts
to be compensated by the view: so you go back

to your clumsy manoeuvring – and suddenly
there they are, a party of yellowhammers,
tiny gold arrows prickling the air, angling
into sharp corners, taking deceptive bends

at full tilt (not using left lane but passing),
performing a perfectly slick little comedy,
anarchy choreographed, glint of summer
on a lacklustre day. But you notice,

however they flourish those trim kites
of light, they don't monkey about with
the road. There are ways, so they say,
of taking your life in your hands.

The outward and visible signs

'We are great readers here, and we passed
your new book round like a stone that glints
in the light; but I thought, this cannot say
if my old friend is well, happy. . . .
Tell me, how are things with you?'

I fold up the letter, not knowing how to reply,
then I remember the gourd – no, it is
a baobab fruit, but very like a gourd;
a young man in the Fremantle Market had brought it
down from the north, the lizard designs
delicately carved on the surface
by the Aborigines up there in the village.

It is beautiful and rare, a large enough oval
to hold in your cupped hands, light and dry
to the touch. When you shake it the kernel inside
rattles against its walls. 'In time'
said the young man 'the kernel will dry up
to nothing, then the shell is ready to oil and varnish,
it will shine, and the lizards will seem alive.'

It is true there is nothing to say; I work
alone, I am always writing – but such news is
the rattle of a slow interior drying. I want
my friend to have something finished and formed;
I will send this patterned shell.

Things

Yes, I like it here,
things have their place;
at night there are lights in the water;
if you offered me something unexpected –
a fast car, a bantam hen,
a small bunch of violets
purple velvet and looking authentic,
I would be touched
though I could easily refuse.

I have choices galore
but the same grey trees lean to the wind
at my window,
the same unwary bird is killed
every day on the grass,
and I long to long for something attainable
by sheer hard work
– like cars or clothes –

whatever would not, when achieved,
stay in its place looking perfect
with death's shadow
slowly deepening
behind it.

The Real Estate

for C.E.B.

Every building is a bid to find
the long way home where all
are homeless: that machine across the valley
gouging the hillside with its claws of steel
has somewhere still this early mild intention;

here, there's equivocal fulfilment:
on a rainy Saturday a shut door,
ticking clock, rows of canisters of tea,
the sleeping cat, can all delude me
with their placid emanations of belonging.

And there's the other life that leans its head
against the very earth itself, takes caves
and knotted branches, fires on the beach,
a desert camp, as kitchens to the soul,
pauses in the long uncomforted meandering.

Look, you despise him for his greed, but
the property developer frowning at midnight
at his phosphorescent figures on the screen
is one with you on the mountainside or her or me
in rooms cat-coddled, children-comforted:

silence awaits us all. What's more I think
the oldest of us wants it so, not just in resignation:
what gods there are that stalk the bleak heaths
of eternity might yearn for even these
implausible retreats, our finite anchorage.

Doubletake

I saw without looking flamingos were flying,
pohutukawas doing cartwheels over the hill,
the garden full of gazelles, dancing for sure . . .

then it was daylight, morning; Thursday;
your pillow slightly dented, spectacles left
by the bed, your special smell. I looked out,

saw a crimson launch stooging over the harbour,
two starlings in the pine tree, an orange arctotis
in bloom by the path – but everything queerly bright,

so I stared in disbelief. And I suddenly thought,
gazelles, etc., are OK: this is love's greater
invention, that it can take a red boat,

gossipy birds, an ancient familiar daisy, and
remake them, leaving all things their familiarity,
giving each a surpassing strangeness.

At the Exhibition: 'Gun Club', Eion Stevens

It's up on the wall, the rifle –
not loaded, very black against that
great thunder of scarlet; reminder
of a prowess as big as battalions
that afterwards drifted away.

It shows in the back of his cropped head,
the smallest slump in the shoulders –
Ladies' Night – and she's there all right
sitting opposite, plain, rather blank,
finding the company awkward,

puzzled at coldness in this convivial room
– yet he asked her to come,
'share his interests', see how in harmless
husbandly fashion he's occupied
Wednesday nights – and she does see,

smiles and shivers, 'Yes, I am having
a good time. Interesting . . .',
(the targets, the trophies) and stares
at his square fingers holding the glass
tight, like a toy; like a trigger.

City Lights

for Anne French

On a still evening you stare at the sea's glistening
till it calls up the sheen of that more or less oval pool

of light on your bent knee as you sat marvelling
at taffeta and sophistication at seventeen say, or eighteen,

and had to stroke it in wonder till it merged into
the whole temple of light you had so gloriously become.

Now as you watch the gleam separates without moving
into needles, stilettos, rapiers, points plunging down

as they form, till the whole darkening body of the sea
is deeply, brilliantly divided. Light on the surface

has produced a total internal exposure. As for the city
that turns on the current, it lies as always out of reach.

You took your hand away of course from that wondering
caress, to dance the two-step – or was it a waltz –

pursuing the light on the arrived moment towards
impossible fulfilments, unimagined treacheries.

In the end you don't see the city at all, only
the reflections stabbing the motionless water.

Anorexic Girl

If she could only fly, the sick girl, let
her light limbs take her away and away, so
the pestering solicitude of parents and nurses
can no longer hang like a hot dress in summer
over her flimsy body, thin-angled shoulders –

can they not hear her disgust at their talk
of giant eating, slurp of eggs, bread,
overripe fruit, thick cake . . . she turns
from them painfully, devoured by
the great hungers nobody will acknowledge –

and remembers the Indian girl in the store
at the corner, how her tired eyes shine
in their purple shadows as she speaks
of parcels sent to the brother she hardly knows
in Calcutta . . . how she can never stay,

being carried away by the wide tide of work
the urgent, the necessary work. *These patients
had a golden childhood from which they cannot escape*
notes the doctor; but the Indian girl
moved straight into the cold clinic of hardship

– there like rough linen close to the skin
ride the purposed denials, the exhaustion,
the celebration at news of the families – ah
the thing needful, the strong hand enclosing
the soul; its ancient, forgotten food.

Prayer to Cydippe, Priestess to Hera

Madam let me never be unsurprised

never suppose as I reach towards
the morning I have deserved
its strange and reckless shining:

let me realize it slowly, like
the sharp taste of the fleshy cells of an orange

teach me how to befriend the strangers
who stand in the eyes of the men and women
who are my children

pray for me priestess now and at the hour
of my failure; when I am blind
to the lizard-flick of the lie beneath
truth's whitened stone, destroy my comfort
send me into the dark till I am lost, hurt
betrayed but for the precarious accidents
of love

Handmaiden to the imperfect goddess
walk with me
through this temple of earth and sky
this clearing
in the incomprehensible jungle

as its constantly altering pathways grow shorter
let me not imagine arrival in one place
or another
O Lady of risk and caprice, only by this
shall I confront my end
in proper nakedness, as I began.

The Hour

for H.W.

It's happened again,
subtle rustling, the tuning up
of invisible small birds
abroad in the darkening bush,
same six o'clock, still point
in a season of flux,

boats soundlessly drawing their triangles
over a grey page of sea,
secret flight of the clouds
and I here waiting, to tell you

– you only, so I ask: is this love,
this visible sheen
on a minor time, half an hour, less,
of a random twenty-four, and you
in it with me? Love surely
is accommodations, struggle,
rages understood and survived,
a forgiving wisdom –

yes, true. But even failed lovers are permitted
their moments – listen: a faint rasping
of strings, tiny exquisite music
that will die with the dark, an echo
of old six o'clocks . . . all the six o'clocks
in the history of the world, let's say,
in a single half hour. Take it, be quick –
sunset you know is already beginning
to make havoc of things
on the hills.

The Problems of the Articulate Middle Classes

I step round my solitude with a scrupulous lightness
I am afraid of disturbing its sleeping bulk
stretched out over my room
I have scarcely an inch to squeeze past:
it only lay down a moment ago
just as the last person went out the door
and I want it to stay there
eyes shut and not stirring
for hours and hours and hours.

We began with politics I believe, especially opinion polls
    (approximately 20 minutes)
followed by a proper crescendo of responsible minority indignation
    (25)
the vulgar ambitions of rich developers who sponsor the nation's
    culture and probably debase it (nearly 45)
a good book written by a friend (10)
disclosures of amazing disloyalty perpetrated by someone's respected
    colleague (1 hour)
who's also a friend (half)
and promiscuous as well (right through to 6.30)
the despair puzzlement and recurring dislocation of
                the young (40 minutes)
                the old (15)
                ourselves (all day and
                          the day before and
                                the day after)
and in between these archaeology and architecture and
administrative obsession and Aids and solitude and slimming
and cervical cancer and systems analysis and poetry and post-
holocaust novels and other dead serious and marginally
significant interweavings of themes and variations and
linguistic proliferations
we can
excite
in
one
another.

Now if I reduce myself to a shadow, a thinness, scarcely a
breath,
the motionless shape on the floor
will go down, down, into a truly profound unconsciousness
and I will sit still
and wait
and at last, very faintly and from far away in the distance
will perhaps come to my ears
the wordless and meaningless
exquisitely musical
song of the silence.

By Appointment

Cameras, contraptions and charming people
came into my house and tapped me on the shoulder
saying 'Take us to it, the source,
the inscrutable image, what it is your soul
reaches towards as bodies lean to the sun . . .'

and I agreed, saying eagerly 'here' and 'here'
bent myself over the mysterious page
again and again ('take one' 'take four') – and
truly I have my reward, thirty pieces
of vivid half-knowledge publicly possessed;

also my punishment, now I return to
my re-ordered room and photogenically
disarranged desk to find silence dead as the earth
in a dry well and my haunting, elusive, maddening
mercurial voices refusing to utter a word.

Sober Truth

for Hone Tuwhare

It's a sharp morning, sea and city
tipped to acutest angles; bare roots of the ngaio
tie the clay bank in knots,
the stark edge of building cranes
slices the distance – nothing gives,
except perhaps in my head where last night's
celebration slides like a heavy sack
over the floor when I bend.

I'll sit here
on the cracked asphalt margin of the bush path,
feet on the crumbly dirt, wind and shadow
settling quietly down beside me
to write you a letter, old mate, rascally charmer,
your bumble-bee voice still brushing my ear
with the whirring
of incorrigible whisperings.

Each of us lives in the body differently.
Yours is a total occupation, Full House
to the last crease and capillary, the quick
of the smallest toe-nail, each follicle and fibre,
to the fingers that tingle with mischief
and magic as they move the pen
over your own page, your poems.

Yes, you're yourself all the way through,
the breathing radiator I've often stood near
in a spell of hard weather of the heart,
warmed by some great buzz
of laughter and love at the centre.
This, old friend, is to tell you
I got safely home last night
after the party.

Death by Accident

I hear it first in her, the slow perplexity
that does not know a vocabulary of loss.
Women move about her kitchen making tea,

one irons a shirt; 'You go upstairs and sit
with him' she says, 'not many have come who were
especially for him.' And there in a study

stalled in a paper-filled untidiness,
he sits alone; tells me how the boy could make
his brother laugh, made friends with girls

who always fell for him; then she's at the door
with tea for him – 'Have it with the whisky.'
It's a later marriage, he's learnt the fatherhood

of sons quite recently, shows now a shuddering
half-acknowledged pain: 'It's her I think about.'
Like children, hand in hand they go

to their sorrow, as though they knew that
in death's vast disorder only their small
habitual kindnesses will survive.

The Visit

They say we are to leave. An hour,
no more, and we go back where we may choose
and change, follow sudden impulse, find ourselves
surprised. And you? Because of us

you feel again the force of being here,
here still tonight, tomorrow, every morning
when you wake: *Prison*, how it hammers at us,
beats like fists no matter how we move together,

close up chairs to make a circle, laugh, agree.
All the time we read our gently hopeful poems
it is marching up and down the room
behind our backs and shouting at us.

Yet, and yet, just as loud are voices shouting
that we are the same – sixteen of you, we two;
your bodies burn like ours with unattended lusts,
your breasts can hold a weight of milk, your arms

support a man, a child, easily like us you will
forgive, you understand a woman's willingness
for pain; beyond your quarrelling, your rage
you know all our temptations, our defeats.

And yes of course you know all that –
how kind you are, how tactfully you keep from us
the crowding spectres as, grossly rich, we blunder
through your poverty. How you protect us,

waving when the gate clangs shut, smile
to release us as we take our convict selves away
past the dark paddocks, silent with each other
in the car, all the way to town.

Late Dinner

Moving uncertainly among cups and glasses,
flowers and windows, you are changed tonight
– small, and shaken, as though just now
dropped from the great beak of destiny
as it swooped low over the earth,
done with you, not caring to notice (as though
it ever does) the hard grass,
the irregular hidden stones. Yes, I will have

ice, and cream with the pears, the fire up,
or not . . . the wine too is sufficiently dry
oh my dear how are we to speak of your thin
covering, the everlasting expanse of the plain
and the violent sky, the keening of the wind, –
how shall I tell you these are just
the expected wearinesses, the wind sings merely
of the grass, and its rootedness in the earth

– and it will hurt much less if you don't
thresh about like that. Come down now,
let the cruel wings move away
while you settle yourself in a hollow; here,
give me your glass, it is a little water
you need. Long as the journey was, and wonderful
the mountains and seas, the ledges where you
were almost devoured precarious and strange,

still this rolling easy plain all around you
is only a place, which is to say, no place;
and the silence that looms up beside you,
look you now quietly, it is only death.

The Night Burns with a White Fire

The night burns with a white fire
and the moths move silently
among the moon flowers; I see her
in the garden standing quite still
beyond the blurred darkness of the fig tree
smiling a little, her pale face
familiar but smaller than I remember it.
I cannot go to her; the Acheron,
river of sorrow, lies between us,
and the moon flowers' unearthly forebodings.

The Czech Girl

Consider the classroom – 'Laughing Cavalier'
on the wall, smell of sweat and grimy
woodwork, half-open windows fracturing
the afternoon – and the shy Czech girl,
good at Chemistry, hampered by lack
of English; could she thank the foreign
visitor in his language? We crowd
close to her – a short speech perhaps?

She hesitates, smiles at our eager faces
– and it does please the burly Russian,
he is exuberant, tells of his brother
garrisoned in Prague, explains
the Soviet attitude: we argue freely
– this is a truly liberal exchange
of views. Now Anya will speak for us:
proudly we watch her walk forward. . . .

It was seven years ago. Today I am
in Prague myself, in a small restaurant
in the old city – we walked here through
crooked, cobbled streets; the wine
is good, you are talking in excellent English
of poems you write that your people
will never read; translated,
you can publish some things abroad. . . .

Your voice is dry, dispassionate,
you will not allow me to pity you –
but your eyes, your eyes! There I see her
again, the Czech girl; she rises
from their dark shadows and again
she is running, running through
a forgotten classroom door
in a storm of inconsolable weeping.

Poem for Carlos

Clambering across rough turf in the five o'clock
autumn chill, I think of you curled up in there,
mouse-sized kitten, bird naked beneath
the enveloping feathers, pouched kangaroo, you
twenty-inch parcel of boy, sleeping so hard you frown
with the serious business of being a baby.

Out here stand the giant crags, the river,
the yellowing poplars marching over the spurs,
the toi-toi and billowing pasture and, close enough
to touch here in the valley, a huge horizon
of hills; after, a changeless vigil
of stars . . . all that waits for your growing,

your playing and working, your time of staunchness
and strength, hands bloodied at the killing
of a sheep or patient in gentling a young dog,
a horse, time for the dry days of planting
and harvesting, time even for leaving . . .
I walk back to the yellow window,

come in to your quiet capsule of a room,
close the door. For the moment it's to stay
outside, the cold dusk, the great sky ripening now
as though with the complex lustre of lifetimes,
the rocks towering over the house, dark with
their secrets of future valiant surmountings.

Road Works

In this street that has ignored so many
poignant or desperate encounters
I may meet my angry daughter. Will she smile,
speak? Would she brush past?

I blush at my imagined confusion; I who
am too old to be awkward, too long tried
to be shy, become clumsy before
the urgent legitimate rage of the young.

Today the whole world has not allowable space
for us both. I loiter, hesitate, one of those
seen peering through street barricades
trying to make out the movements

of workers inside. Does she lean, press,
straighten and bend as, back turned, fired
by a furious assurance, she piles up
the fragile sandbags of the future?

A Two-Year-Old Considers Pregnancy in Parents

The way she goes on you'd think her bulge
was the only one in the world
oh I know she claims she's got hold of a baby
caught it out of the air as it flew
holed it up in there so the rest of us
can't see its silly face or anything

doesn't she know there are ways –
look at me for example with my fat mangy teddy
and Meg and Mog
and a yoghurt sandwich
and my Dad singing a song
and Hokianga Harbour
and an enormous high bridge of red blocks that doesn't fall over
and a long squeeze of blue jelly toothpaste
and a picked daffodil
and a blue unburstable balloon
and a soft corner of my cuddle-rug
and a ripe strawberry
and a star
and rolled up together so I shiver and sparkle
with the quivering all-purpose magic of things nesting
inside me; they don't even take up much room
they are secret as first light
and big as the dark
with a funny strong interesting smell –
I think it's of mothers.

Really

for George

Where you are, nobody was before.
It was a gap in the texture of things,
it did not echo
nor shimmer
nor tingle
nor in any way make itself present or visible,
in fact it wasn't anything; it did not wait for you,
it did not even imply light enough
for us to call it transparent –
we did not know it was there
till you entered it
gave it shape and smell (new skin,
cells, blood of the early world),
you made it look like small arms and legs
and eyelids, it sounded like breathing –

now you will possess it always, that is to say
for a long time
till it tires you out
and grows old and slack anyway;
right now it fits you beautifully, your reality,
I like you in it; hello.

Family Group

The children of the family are playing families:
cousins brought up by the touchy sisters exhibit
judicious bossiness the little ones swallow whole;
the smallest shivers with ecstasy merely at being
included by this beneficent authority. The sun
is hot on the hills: here by the walnut trees
we will light a fire in the evening, eat out on the grass.

Conversations bloom all about with instant colour
like nasturtiums sown in the wind. We have all
travelled a long way. The old jokes are heard
in echoes and fragments, as we see forgotten summers
in the crumpled rugs on the grass.
And of course she is here too, the one who
for ten years has set us the hardest lesson –

to find what it is even death cannot take away:
I hear a familiar cadence, see a still tenderness,
hand lightly placed on the arm of a tired young
husband, some poise in a seated figure –
these are the blends, the trace elements,
the life after death of her, now in our keeping,
mutely alive in our lives, like the threads still

bright in the old tartan rug where we sprawl.
I look round at these figures in a mellow landscape
and know we have passed our meridian; the precious
inheritance is being received, by unconscious
yet deliberate act and moment by moment, into
the proper hands. This is the photograph
of a notable occasion no one remembered to take.

New Poems

Late Home

So, it's like this - footfalls
in a cold street, moon lurking behind
the lurid cloud, your echoes leaping
and snarling at the horizon. 1.30, all

living room lights turned off, garages locked,
you only at large, heels clopping too loudly
past driveways and gates . . . then you
feel them beside you, eerie, invisible,

the millions you know can never go home:
their spectres crowd the suburban street,
they are thin, their eyes knowing and sharp,
they come close, flapping and brushing -

hurry on down the long sloping path
to your door then (your hand shakes while you're
fitting the key); look up at the chairs,
curtains, bookshelves, glowing with use

through the window, receive the warm air
that opens towards you. Go on, shut the door,
plain and quick now. Your gestures exhibit
the exact, furtive prudence of the thief.

Brian

He's everywhere today, verandah, window sill,
back step, coming from nowhere if I open
the fridge door, however quietly; hints of white
blink at the edge of vision when I turn . . .

of course I knew, half knew, yesterday at five
(the hour that's gone *ping* in his brain, or
his digestion – and which was which, for him? –
these fourteen years); he stood up stiffly

from his patch of shade, and slowly, as I
watched and wondered, walked away. Where do
they go, cats? – discreet as spies, no farewells,
no unclean decomposition; just the silence,

sharp, as this one is, with a thousand
conversations, the taste and smell of little pieces
of our lives: they stuck to him, I think,
he carried them about, sweetened them perhaps,

as though his persistent presence (scattering
exasperating white fur on every chair) was just
the homely disguise selected by a household god
too strange for ordinary folk to look upon.

The Fourth of July

for Alexander Masovianus

Tingling on the secret encompassing wire
comes the current of his voice: 'there are
lights on the boats spread over the water . . .'

(the cold afternoon leaning over my fireplace
rises and turns to listen) '. . . dusk is deepening,
the summer air's clear, and I see that every star

in the sky has fallen into Lake Michigan . . .'
I breathe in, pause, take it up, this pinch
of brilliance, tiny luminous envelope,

carry it out to the winter town. There
I grin at the mystified girl at the bus stop,
at the violinist playing in the Mall (shall I

fill his whole case with silver?), at
the *Evening Post* boy at his corner; even, in
her neutral cubicle, at the doctor; 'nothing wrong

here – or here –' (so, it cures pain too?)
then easily climb the stiff hill to my house,
seeing it shimmer with brand-new constellations.

Ward Island, Lake Ontario

All week it was there – a low fringe on the brow
of the lake: *it's for summer, don't go now
in the snow* . . . but standing about all day
among strangers I thought of it, watched at night,
oh I would be safe there, deep-hidden, alone –

so I stood on a slippery plate of a deck
gripping a rail of black ice in a wind that came
slicing over a continent, ice all the way;
our expressions, our squeezed-out syllables
shrivelled, set solid; became air ice.

On the thin streets, stiff little cottages
all porches and gables, toys left out in the snow,
a few children stout in their padding, the lads
playing ice hockey on the lagoon; on the boardwalk
gulls landed and slid, then stepped precisely;

at the jetty, families were coming home laughing,
jostling as the moorings were slung, women
with supermarket trolleys, a man humping a basket
of bottles and bread; Saturday shopping; daily living.
It wasn't 'my island' at all. It's theirs; it's theirs.

Visiting Worser Bay School on Sunday Morning

Honeysuckle, taupata, rangiora, briar rose,
the usual Wellington tangle spreading over
the usual hill, steep to the sea; behind me

the school in its soughing pines – and pohutukawas
which also sing to the wind, but not with the aching cry
of the pines. All as it was. Forty years since I

bustled about (I suppose that's what I did)
in these hilltop classrooms, while the amiable
lazy headmaster went off playing golf or bowls.

Hard to believe these moving fictions of time, here
by the sea and the white-shouldered crags, smell
of roots and the salt whiff up from the beach –

even the rebuilt school is the same (there will always
be children). Mine alone is a single season; one spring,
one winter. So. Did I come searching for signs? I see

the years' indifference, prodigal, casual, calm;
the fine ease of growth and decay – and you know
I am oddly released by it. Leaning here, high over

the old tide's patient repetitions, I find myself
smiling and asking, was it forty years, truly,
or four, or – have I forgotten? – four hundred?

Breakdown

We lean over the brink together,
gaze into the greasy dark, one

each side, frowning. 'Don't think
it's the battery,' he mutters, 'try

the ignition –' *Yah shore*: my tone's
neutral, deep, no woman's cadences here,

this is jokers' talk. Like a four-year-old
in high heels, I'm in love with my nonchalance;

How far d'yer reckon she'll go? – my face
and body do it deadpan. Mine is

a sophistication too fine for shrugging
and such excess; don't care for the answers

either – I'm listening for the applause. I've
got an audience of one, and it's not him.

Biography

I saw a small she-goat, skin tight
over her bony frame, and sharply white
among clumps of dun grass on the hill;

I admired the delicate angle of her head
and thought of her usefulness – all day
eating that scraggy stuff (with summer,

the fire season, on the way) and now
digesting it sensibly in the pale, late light
of afternoon. A good creature, fitting

her own rules to ours. I liked her so much
it hardly mattered that when I came round
the hill again there was only a white plastic

bag hung ballooning over a thistle stalk
up there. It was short then, my little
goat's life and work. But ah, glorious.

The Heap

Grey scales on flat slab faces, awkward edges
where the axe came in this side or that –
chunks, blocks, bits, they don't even smell
like wood. Thick cracked peelings scrape off
when I heave the heavy lumps. Grass that travelled
through the chinks falls, colourless and frail;

but the dust is magical – dense festooning clouds
in a gossamer of insect skeletons and grains,
old leaves, the nameless populations of ten years
of wind and sun and rain. Ten years! Almost
too strange to think about, the deep changing,
the turning of that enormous wheel to which

our lives know only they must somehow cling.
It was the dismemberment of macrocarpa,
stickyberry, pine, that used to shade this end
of the house; stacked for fires, shared fires
in the confident rooms where we would spend
the long inconsequential privacies of middle age.

There's no sound in the house; the bottom logs
are gone; resting on the ground I look into the piles
of dusty stuff, take handfuls of it – look,
how curiously it holds together, tangible clouds
veined still by threads from glands of spiders –
generations dead, decayed or long since gone away.

The Task

Death is the signal, the summoning – all those
scattered ones now to come back to the house:

the child in the corner behind the delphiniums
patting the ground to sit down, talking softly

to ghosts and dolls; the girl who chuckled
and grinned, the grave-eyed young woman,

small hands turned out at the wrists,
walking precisely into a room aromatic

with potted origanum and mint; the still figure
in the ward, drawn already away into silences

too remote for mother or sister or lover.
Look, look at them, look through your tears –

this is your test, to find in your hurt heart
the door, the threshold, the dry timber

of walls and verandahs, the creaking of stalks
in the autumn garden; all this, her home now for ever.

Anniversary

The white rhododendron has come into flower
– one glistening cluster, ripe and virginal
at the same time; it's grown too, in the year
it's been marking the spot – yours, we said,
walking across to it under the apple trees carrying
our glasses of wine – 'yes, this is the place',
and I think we each did a bit with a trowel.

It wasn't the last word, though – you're here now
in the dusk, laughing somewhere behind me
at what you still had in store for us . . . but
it's so domestic! Look at me bending down
taking the spoon – a tablespoon (nothing paltry
about this measure) out of the box of . . . well,
look, it's you, isn't it, this white pile –

why do they call it ashes? My dear, you are grit,
all through; you rattle, you tinkle, as I take
one, two, good spoonfuls of you. It's hilarious
I can see, for the doubled-up ghost of you
over there under the trees, purged of this
heavy stuff, watching me, pointing out
how familiar it is, this kitcheny action –

after all, most of our time was in kitchens,
talking – or shouting – among cooking and kids,
running a complex show and keeping our spirits up,
eager, or cynical, or frivolous – dog-tired too,
of course. Under the leaves, that white sprinkle
gleams in the darkening garden. Remember the day . . .
oh to hell with it. I wish you were here.

Long Distance

The small enveloping question
Are you all right? your voice
twisting latitudes of air into
that tiny syllabic skein. The line

clicks, pauses, distance catching
us up – and I without an answer;
daily I lose my footing, the great
wheels grind over; I am rolled,

crushed, stung by grim words, yet
restored by a lift of the light
through trees in a summer dusk; know
the precarious joy beyond a hail

of pain. This is my weather, my
condition. My words tremble into
the tunnelling dark. As for *all right*
– I will never be more so. Or less.

Illness

Shut the door quickly let them not come for me
walking up from the river through the willow trees
where last night I saw floating the distracted faces
of my children like flowers on the water.

Let them not confront me emphatically
or walk with me along the footpath where old men
lean over sagging fences, nor hurry me
into a car holding my wrists too hard
with their big washed hands.

I remember the time when I took off
my shoes and lay down on the road to taste
the great green fruit of the sky, there were
clouds like white apples and far back
in the house I heard with surprise
the wild voices of the children crying.

Pas de Deux

We kiss, coolly; somewhere you can hear
a light wrench like the tearing of old rag.
Don't listen – we're impeccable,

fit for each solemn tedious abstraction:
'balance' 'recognition' 'compromise'.
We're labourers in fact, lackeys, we who once

ran the outfit, and with such panache.
Remember the day . . . that crumbly pie . . . the way
we laughed . . . the exquisite clumsiness . . .

No, no, not that lost aristocratic dialect! It's
failure's strict vocabulary – 'divorce – dividing –
whoever should die first – '. The room is shrinking

by the minute, as though to fit two small
dull creatures, no more now than human size.
Outside though is huge, an aching universe,

the suburban garden spinning like a frozen plain,
the sky a broken opal fired by a sick old sun
too weak to warm one single footprint to the gate.

Dog

A dog barking far off
at fall of dusk
over and over repeating its muffled
unrelenting message,
filling you with foreboding –

useless now to wish you had accepted
that last invitation, boring as it was,
or joined the neighbourhood protest,
had a swim, even, with young Julia,
agreed to count votes in the hall – oh really,

as though we *want* it like this,
this living! Of course there are better
ways, people have them –

trouble is, you get home to
the pure essence, the moment,
and here's this dog with its awful barking,
sorrow upon sorrow
across the diminishing afternoon.

Stone Seal to Stone Owl

Faint as our voices are – mere impulses
in the nervous system of the world, whose networks
infinitely proliferate between us – I
salute you: friend, tiny solid creature,
shaped rock of almost luminous grey (to my
mottled green) with your round and solemn eyes,
where mine are glossy slits – you were carried
east, I south. We shall not meet again
beneath the chisel of a common hand.

But we can prove our place, mute cells
in the chain of being, by sending and receiving,
thus, a ripple of meaning from the nuggets
of energy we are – you on your shelf
in an English living room, I squinting in
the hot late summer sun of a room that looks
across the bay to Wellington, twelve thousand miles
of seas and continents away. Dear owl,
this is to celebrate the scientists' news

that the trembling planet in its deepest
resonance – the place of neutrons
and electrons and their parts – is not made up
of things, not particles at all, but action,
thought, response, relationship. We live
by our connections. And so the soundless messages
that spin between us, even us, two little fists
of living stone, are beautiful as music
of the spheres, essential units in
the moving pageant of the universe.

Dialogue

You write from your farm in Zambia;
your African wife (who sends me messages)
I have never seen; but I too read

in my accustomed place, a window over
a small cold sea, eight thousand miles
to the south-east. Your voice, matter-of-fact

and sane, could be a phone call from someone
near at hand, though you speak of mammoth
events. 'In South Africa the train to freedom

is leaving the terminus at last . . . we have
little news; riots, broken glass . . .' Then
you proceed, with the scholar's fanatic

patience, to explain the Portuguese slave
trade, three hundred years ago; assuming,
as a friend should, that what ignites

your attention is for the moment mine too.
We are sharing a world, a history; when you
recall Donne's 'round earth's imagined corners'

once again knowledge itself explodes as an act
of imagination, as a fire, a song. Here,
the spring afternoon follows rain, starlings

shriek and laugh in the high birch trees.
Friend, working in your hot blood-damaged
continent, come outside with me; listen –

that softly lyrical clashing and scraping,
the cool drip of the leaves: they are yours
now. I honour one gift with another.

Academic Honours

They made speeches, they clothed me in robes;
in their eager excitement they made themselves
beautiful. In the morning I opened the car door

and carefully placed the fine creature
I had with me over the passenger seat –
scarlet gown (post office box red, in fact),

tasselled black velvet cap, pink satin lining
caressing the slinky hood. 'My God you are
splendid,' I remarked, 'sure it's OK if I

get in?' And then all the way into town
I practised one of my special offhand
expressions I do when no one is watching.

Writing on the Wall

GENERALS: LOVE NEVER DIES; A MOMENT
OF DARKNESS WILL NOT MAKE US BLIND.
It's scrawled in big letters on a sign

outside Pablo Neruda's house at Isla Negra on
the Chilean coast. Listen to it – do the hundred
degrees of longitude that divide us from

South America distort the pitch? It comes
quaintly; is that what they found deep down,
after Pinochet's killings, a vein of

passionate hope, innocence even, a mad
longing? Our graffiti is younger, more raw,
addressed to Ladies and Gentlemen, cowboys,

tycoons – we don't have generals; the army
doesn't kill us at present. The story here
is richest is best and to hell with the rest,

shooting and kicking around can stay in
the kitchen. We're kids really, greedy and rough.
Do we need a few lessons? Kids do, to grow up.

Midwife

'It's time' one of us breathes into the phone
– but she knows, she's already here putting down
her bag of mysteries (oxygen mask? forceps?)

and the chief performer, first violin, the star,
takes her position; as for the rest of us,
well, we know a maestro when we see one –

she's the one with the supple wrist; easy,
precise, she coaxes us into our parts,
we'd follow her anywhere – when she's ready

for us to move forward, aside, we know by
a particular intentness of fingers and face
that draws us in to the whole resonant magic:

and then we're there – all, even the extras,
have come to a brilliant finale. She steps down,
congratulating the lead (there are two of them now),

us too – and yes, thank you, she will have a glass
of champagne – as though she's done nothing
special. Now that's skill. That's style.

Pohutukawa

Red; blood-red. Crimson wreaths upon
the branches' royal architraves; stained-
glass sun, sharp against the harbour.

In here, the ghosts of other years,
forgotten festivals – spilt wine, tears,
violent laughter in another room – and

beyond all that the thinner shades, of pagan
gods against their fir tree snow, spring
stirring in the frozen northern ground.

What could we do? We fashioned other idols
– like Guy Fawkes, stuffed with straw – and,
pointing, said 'the family'; 'You must come

home for Christmas.' So it is. We do not know
if we recall, or simply now imagine, that small
eternity of love, a kitchen couch, a clover-

scented paddock . . . But every year across
the summer country pilgrimages move towards their
illusory shrine, and there in eating, spending,

rioting, we search for grace; and rub our little
griefs till, tinder-dry, they flare to quarrelling.
Outside there is no cold astringent winter air,

but railway platforms, risky highways, fake
affection's sour taste in the heart; the trees.
Needles of blood are falling through the rain.

Lake Idyll

for Frances

Mount Tauhara, substantial as it is,
rose in the afternoon and settled,
poised without effort in a blue breath
of air, lake water, the remote snows

of Ruapehu: all blue. Gravity itself
became a sheeny vapour that entered
and transmuted every rock and scree
till earth flowered into light.

'Will you stay,' she said '– leave tomorrow
morning?' And at once arrangements, work
the clotted bulk that leans against
the days entered that rapt atmospheric

alchemy and was dissolved. All night
the water lapped outside my window,
new worlds forming hour by subtle hour
in movements of its liquid particles.

5 P.M. December 29

Inscrutable mite of a one-minute life,
grey-blue as from an earlier element,
– earth – water – now you are trying air,
tasting the world like a drop on a spoon –

we are the ones in tumult, laughing and
crying (were we expecting a mouse then,
a kitten?), dancing about *Look! it's
a boy!* – and truly we did talk of girls;

but you, clever thing, knew all along, you
were a boy way back in April and only decided
today to let on; I expect you have plans for
the next half-century too, lying back there

turning yourself oxygen-pink: you're the newest
person there is, little Adam, you come bearing
the aeons in with you, and their matchless
secret, the mystical art of beginning again.

Subliminal

So like him, and so cruelly unlike, this
pale thing dressed up in the grey suit,
white shirt, dark tie he always chose for
funerals – presumptuous facsimile, no more;
I hate its spurious command, its way of
claiming, hour by wordless hour, to be

the version authorised, the only one extant.
How could my friend agree to such diminishment?
A sort of rage possesses me – yet as the silence
perseveres, its very changelessness begins a change
in me: I look again, and see the aching shadow
of his age, the walking stick he didn't like,

the paling eyes; and further back, the younger,
sharper man he used to be. It's living itself
that weakens all our faculties; how little
in the end could he remember even what they were,
the sunlit future promises of long ago. I want
to say 'Hard going, then?' and take his hand.

But suddenly, as though he's heard and answered
me, I know there's something else, a pleasure
– yes, almost – in finding at last you do not have
to take another single breath. Now I can
touch his cold unnatural skin quite easily.
It's not so very different from my own.